Anthony Burton

The Miners

Anthony Burton
The Miners

ANDRÉ DEUTSCH

First published by André Deutsch Limited
105 Great Russell Street   London WCI

Copyright © 1976 by Anthony Burton

Arrangements of photographs and drawings © by
Conway Picture Library Limited 1976

Designed by Mike Jarvis

This edition published by arrangement with Futura
Publications Limited

Printed in Great Britain by Jarrold and Sons Ltd, Norwich

ISBN 0 233 96727 3

Contents

Chapter One
Pit Visit 7
   The Early Days 14
Chapter Two
The First Deep Mines 25
Chapter Three
The Two Wars 37
   Working The Mines 48
Chapter Four
The First Unions 65
Chapter Five
Men, Women and Children 73
   Away Home 85
Chapter Six
The Search for Unity 91
   Accident and Disaster 104
Chapter Seven
The Search for Safety 113
   Struggle 122
Chapter Eight
Union 131
   Time off 141
Chapter Nine
Below Ground and Above 145
   Miner 153
Chapter Ten
Depression and War 161
Chapter Eleven
Mines for the Nation 169

Chapter One
Pit Visit

Hucknall Colliery, Nottingham, early on a summer morning: turning off a busy street straight into the colliery yard is something of an anticlimax. The buildings are modern, anonymous, functional; only the busily spinning wheels of the headstock gear above the shaft, and the familiar and distinctive shapes of the tubs running on their narrow rails to and from the shaft indicate that this is in fact a colliery and not the home of some light industry. 'It wasn't always like this', a colliery official remembers. 'It used to be like something out of D. H. Lawrence, all red-brick offices with 40 watt bulbs. The yard was a mess.' But not now. At this, one of the most modern collieries in Britain, everything is neatness and order, arranged in a logical sequence to ensure maximum efficiency. After the preliminary introduction, however, the realities of mining become apparent.

There is something sobering about being issued with a survival kit, which the demonstrator informs you is to be used after an explosion. It is the seriousness with which safety is treated – 'if we ever forget the dangers of mining, we're done for' – that helps to bring home the reality that underlies the statistics of colliery accidents. The kit consists of a respirator that will give the miner two hours' freedom to breathe in an atmosphere which, after an explosion, would be laden with carbon monoxide. Changing into dirty clothes and pit boots, you go off to collect helmet, lamp, and respirator and pass through the first of the safety checks. At the head of the shaft you hand in a metal tab that is the record that you are going underground. Then you get a last check over, which includes a quick frisking, of exactly the sort seen in a hundred cops and robbers movies, to make sure you have no matches, lighter, or anything else that could spark off an explosion. Then you step into the cage, the wire screen is rolled down, and you hurtle downwards, ears popping wildly.

Underground now, you are still a long way from D. H. Lawrence territory – no cramped roadways here, but a long tunnel lit by fluorescent tubes, just like London Underground without the posters, and marginally cleaner. The first surprise for the visitor unused to underground workings is the cool wind of almost gale-force proportions. This wind is the result of the mine's ventilation system: a powerful fan pulls air up the upshaft, so that fresh, cool air is dragged down the downshaft to pass through the miles of underground workings, along a route determined by a series of heavy wooden doors that prevents the air taking short cuts. As you turn across to another roadway near the foot of the upshaft, the effect on the air of its long journey through the workings is at once dramatically evident. The wind is hardly less strong, but now it is hot and heavily oppressive with a stale smell to it.

The journey to the face starts in style with a ride by conveyor belt, a curious experience, producing a sensation that one imagines to be rather like using a vibrator at a massage parlour. You lie full length on the belt, and every few seconds you receive a jolt as you pass over a roller. From the end of the belt you walk, an opportunity now to exchange a few words with the underground workers. First reactions are predictable. When they know they are talking to someone writing about the mines and miners, they laugh and say 'overworked and underpaid': it comes to sound like an incantation. Then another theme emerges – everyone wants to talk about the past. No, they tell you, they would never want to go back to the old days, the old conditions, but . . . following that 'but' comes something very like nostalgia. The new machines have lightened the load, but they have taken away something of the pride of men who performed prodigious feats of strength in all but impossible conditions. 'This lot,' says a miner in his sixties, 'they'd never last in the old pits.' Time and again, reference is made to the soft seam, 2 foot 10 inches high. 'My father was 6 foot tall, weighed 16 stone, took a size 18 collar. When I first went down, I thought he'd never get in the seam, but he just threw his belly up and climbed in after it.' The penalty to be paid for labour-saving machinery is a certain monotony and a certain loss of independence. Men look back too to the days when what a face worker earned was dependent on what he did. Now, when wages have been evened out, those days are over. The face worker acknowledges that the old system was unfair to the men on day wages, who even if they are not at the face, are an essential part of the team. There is a strong tradition of egalitarianism and comradeship among the men under the ground, stronger they will tell you than in any other industry, but . . . that 'but' is always there, the look back at past times.

The more you talk, the stronger certain impressions become. It is an alien world down here in the mines, and the miners form their own, tight-knit community. For all the fluorescent lights and the new machines, they know that there is always that special risk, the shared danger of the mine. To the visitor it all seems secure in the well-lit roadways, safe enough until someone points to the pipes boring their way into the strata at regular intervals. They carry away the explosive methane gas from the workings, at a rate of several hundred thousand cubic feet each and every working day. And gas is not the only potential explosive: coal-dust itself has been responsible for many, many mining accidents, so that as you walk down the roadways your feet sink into the powdered stone spread to keep the coal-dust down. Then you come upon a section where a part of the roof is being repaired, and men work with picks, attacking the stone. Instead of the comfort of a neat, well-lined tunnel, you are suddenly made conscious of the thousands of tons of rock piled high over this burrow in the ground. This sense of common danger has helped to build the unique sense of comradeship. That and the continuity. You are struck by the age of so many men still working underground, men who have worked down the mines for close on fifty years; men with long memories of their days down the pits, and their fathers', and untold generations before them. It is a continuity of circumstance as much as choice. A miner remembers the 1930s: 'When I left school, my mother didn't want me to go down the pit, so I went to the hosiery factory. I'd been there two weeks when I was called to the manager's office. My cards were on the table. "What's up?" I asked. "Your dad's down pit." "I know that." "Ay, well what's good enough for your dad's good enough for you." So I came down the pit.' Whatever the subject, reminiscence of old times appears.

Somehow the visitor expects life down the pits to be all grimness. In a sense perhaps it is, but there's humour and friendliness as well. One story heard down the pit says a lot about the miner's sense of humour, but rather more about his lack of reverence for bosses. The manager had brought a party of visiting Frenchmen down the pit, and was having difficulty with translation. As he reached the coal-face he shouted out to ask if anyone spoke French. 'Ay,' came a voice from somewhere in the gloom. 'Come out here then.' A black-faced miner appeared from behind a heap of coal, said, 'Do 'ave a Dubonnet,' and disappeared back into the dark. It is said that neither the manager nor the visiting delegation were greatly amused.

Walking along the well-lit roadways, stopping to talk to men along the way, seems hardly more arduous or less comfortable than a walk above ground. Then you reach the face. No lights here, only the light from the lamp on the helmet: turn that light out and there is a total blackness, not the blackness of a dark night at the surface, for even the blackest night contains glimmers of light. But here there is no light. It is as if your head has been covered by a velvet hood. Turning the light on, you move forward to where the men are operating the cutter. In front of them is a heap of shattered coal, piled to the roof. You clamber on hands and knees through a gap between the pile and the tunnel wall and you are at the face itself. Stretching away into the dark distance is the wall of coal. In front of it, rows of hydraulic chocks that can be moved forwards as the face moves forward. There are no drills, pickaxes, or shovels being wielded; the machines have taken over the tasks. Machine cutters and machine loaders – between them they can move more than 10,000 tons of coal from this one face alone. This is a high seam, more than 4 foot of it, but the space left beneath the metal supports still seems uncomfortably limited to someone unaccustomed to working conditions in mines. In front of you, the guide walks with great ease, knees bent, his back almost parallel with the ground. You follow, your helmet beating a staccato rhythm on the roof, like a child running a stick along iron railings. The cutter starts up again, eating its way along the face. Plumes of water are thrown into the air, the coal starts to run past on the conveyor belt. In the light of the lamps, the air seems to be filled with a fine, black rain as coal-dust falls continuously. 'It's the dust you can't see, you have to worry about,' someone remarks laconically. 'That's what gets in your lungs.' Some men wear respirators, but the air at the face is hot and heavy, and the face-masks soon become uncomfortable.

The men who work here, the face workers, are technicians. They no longer spend their days crouching or lying in the seams shovelling coal. Now the machines have taken over, the men are left with the job of tending to the machines. They are technicians just as fitters in a factory are technicians, but with a difference. As a Union representative put it: 'If you're a fitter you expect to get your hands dirty. You'll be dirty up to here.' indicating his elbows. 'In the pit you'll be filthy all over.' To work as a mechanic here, a fitter has to make his way into a dark, confined space. He has to cope with a machine covered in slime and dirt. He has no light apart from his helmet light. Small wonder that many technicians take their training from the National Coal Board – some of the best industrial training to be had – and then take their skills to factory or workshop. As someone remarked, there are only two things that bring men down the pit, better pay and shorter hours. 'Anyone who comes down here because he likes it doesn't belong in pit. He belongs in t'bloody loony bin.'

You make your way along the face, stopping to have a word with the workers, and the same story is repeated – you should have seen it in the old days. Then you clamber out and, thankfully, stand up straight. The shift is over and you wait with the men for the conveyor to the bottom of the shaft. Because there is no smoking underground you find many of the men chewing tobacco or taking snuff as they wait. You get still more stories of the old days. One miner reminisces about the days when there were pit-ponies, and the lads used to race their ponies along the roadways to be first at the cage at the end of a shift – underground Lester Piggotts. When the cage arrives there is a scramble to be in. The doors are closed, the cage whirrs up, and suddenly you are blinking in bright sunlight.

Back at the pit-head baths, the visitor is given the privilege of a private shower. A glimpse of yourself in a mirror gives a shock – black face, black hair, black hands. In the shower the grey water rolls off, seemingly endlessly. Even when you think you must surely be clean, a check in the mirror reveals black lines and streaks and you go back for more washing. You feel not unlike Lady Macbeth, wondering if these hands will 'ne'er be clean'.

Clean at last, and dressed again, there is an opportunity for a last talk with miners and deputies. The same themes emerge: the stories of older days when men worked on contract, being paid for the coal they shifted, able to do the rounds of the pits looking for the best rates; concern about the future of an industry that has suffered too much from changes of policy; the need to get a proper compensation for the working conditions. A final point is made as you go: 'Visitors come round this pit and they see the face, and they say they wouldn't work here, not for a hundred pound a week. Not for a hundred pound. And these are the best conditions anywhere in the country. God knows what they'd say if they saw the others!'

Away from the pit, you remember those working conditions, 'the best in the country', the heat, the discomfort, and, above all, the dust. For the next day, every time you blow your nose you get an unhappy reminder of where that dust lodges. But you remember also the attitudes of the men. There are few industries with a stronger sense of the past, few where present-day attitudes can so clearly be seen to have arisen from the history of the industry, from the war between men and a hostile environment, and the battle to get a decent pay for the men who fight in that war. The story of the coal-miner is the story of the campaigns fought in those two battles.

The Early Days

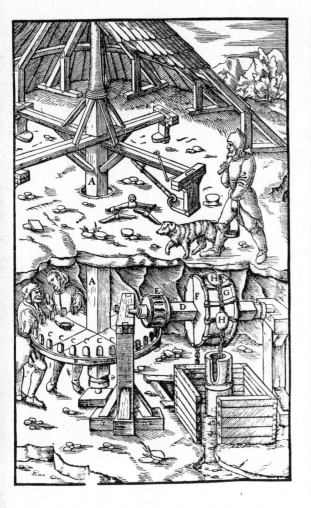

Simple rag and chain pumps kept the workings free of water, though fire risks were not taken very seriously, as is obvious from the miner arriving at work with his lamp. (Agricola)

Haulage could involve the use of the water wheel, though this giant overshot wheel probably owes more to the artist's imagination than to reality. (Agricola)

Opposite: The horse gin used for hauling machinery up and down shafts in the most modern mines, from Agricola's *De Re Metallica* (1556).

Sophisticated machinery did not extend
to transporting the men, who clambered
and slid their way underground.
(Agricola)

Above ground, in the eighteenth century,
the horse whim was still a prominent feature.

Newcomen's steam-engine that ushered in the modern age of mining, enabling men to go down to the deep strata.

The whims form dramatic outlines on the horizon, as here at Pixton Green, Notts.

The movement of coal also brought new sights, as the horse-drawn tram was introduced, running at first on wooden rails.

A late iron tramway near Denby.

It was not all hard work for the horse, which could take advantage of down gradients to get a free ride.

Tramways were the forerunners of the railways, which not only carried coals but used them as well.

EDINBURGH & GLASGOW RAILWAY

COALS

JAMES MACN UGHTON begs leave to inform the habitants of Edinburgh, that he has taken advantage of the facilities afforded by this Railway for bringing into Town, in a fresh state, the COAL of the Redding Coalfield.

The Coals derived from that field are of first quality; and as the Railway affords the means of procuring the Coal fresh from the Pits every day, both in Summer and Winter, J. M. is confident that his Establishment, at the Railway Depot, Hay Market, has only to be tried, to be found to supply an article superior to any yet brought into Edinburgh.

THE FOLLOWING ARE THE PRICES OF SEVERAL OF THE COALS AT THE DEPOT

Duke, of Hamilton's Hard or Splint Coal,	- - -	- - - -	9s. 6d.
Do. Do. Soft Coal,	- -	- - - - -	9s. 6d.
Craigend Splint Coal,	- -	- - - -	9s. 6d.
Do. Soft Coal,	- - -	- - - -	9s. 6d.
Standrig Splint Coal,	- - -	- - - -	9s. 6d.

Cartage, to all places within the Tolls, One Shilling additional.

A rise upon the Price of COALS at the Pits is anticipated very shortly; and Mr MACNAUGHTON recommends Families to supply themselves with COAL before such rise takes place.

Orders sent by Post to JAMES MACNAUGHTON, Edinburgh and Glasgow Railway Depot, or left at the Railway Company's Office, 6 South St Andrew Street; JOHN MACDOUGALL'S, 18 Howe Street; JOHN HILL'S, 60 Broughton Street; SCOUGALL & DRYSDALE'S, 223 High Street; ALEXANDER FERGUSON'S, 1 Melbourne Place; JOHN MACDOUGALL'S, 57 Niddry Street; D. REDPATH'S, 36 Nicolson Street; A. GILLON & SONS', 64 Grassmarket; and R. L. REID'S, 147 Princes Street,---will be punctually attended to.

NOTE.---The Time when the Coals are sent from the Depot is marked on the Railway Company's Ticket of Weight; and Mr MACNAUGHTON requests that any undue delay in delivering the Coals, or any incivility on the part of his Carters or Porters, may be intimated to him.

EDINBURGH AND GLASGOW RAILWAY DEPOT,
Hay Market, October 10, 1842.

James Brydone, Printer, 17 Hanover Street.

By the early nineteenth century, the colliery had taken on many of its distinctive features. T. H. Hair sketched the collieries of the north-east, such as St Lawrence.

Hair's view of Percy Pit, where gas from the workings burned bright over the pit-head.

Below ground conditions were often primitive and brutal. In Scottish mines, the women carried coals on their backs.

Scotswomen hauling coals many hundreds of feet up near-vertical ladders.

The general public knew little or nothing of the underground world until the 1842 Parliamentary Committee on children in the mines published their report, complete with illustrations.

Much publicity was given to the plight of the children.

NOTICE.

NO FEMALES

Permitted, on any account, to work under ground at this Colliery; and all such is **STRICTLY PROHIBITED**, by Orders from His Grace the Duke of Hamilton.

JOHN JOHNSTON, Overseer.

REDDING COLLIERY, 4th March, 1845.   J. Duncan, Printer, Falkirk.

There was a strong movement in favour of banning underground work for women.

'The penitent' – a man who, covered in wet sacking, had the job of exploding the dangerous fire-damp found in many mines.

Chapter Two
The First Deep Mines

The modern mining industry could be said to have begun in the eighteenth century, but the history of mining in Britain goes far back beyond that. As early as the thirteenth century coal was being shipped from the collieries of the Tyne, some of which found its way to the capital. In a document of 1228 a man is referred to as living in 'Sacoles Lane', and Seacoal Lane still exists near the Thames at Ludgate Circus. These earliest workings could hardly be called mines in the modern sense. The first coal was worked where the strata outcropped at the surface, mines being dug horizontally into the hillside to follow the seam. Drift mines of this type still exist, but they are found in very few places. Later another type of mining began. The men would dig a shaft down to the coal-seam and then gradually work their way outwards in all directions from the foot of the shaft. The pits were not very deep and the men could use ladders to climb up and down the shaft, while a simple hand-winch was often all that was necessary to haul up the baskets of coal. Beyond a certain distance from the shaft, the roof of the workings would start to cave in, at which point the miners simply abandoned the workings and sank another shaft down to the seam. The excavated space was similar in shape to a beehive or bell, which gave the name 'bell-pit' to this style of working.

As mining progressed, these primitive techniques became less and less adequate. The miners found they had to dig deeper beneath the surface of the earth to get at the mineral, but as they went down they found themselves faced by one of the miner's many enemies, water. Long drainage channels or adits had to be dug to carry the water away in some places, while in others they resorted to elaborate systems of water-powered pumps. Sir George Bruce, for example, reopened a colliery at Culross in Perthshire which had been thought to be permanently drowned out. He built an Egyptian wheel-pump – a device rather like a modern bucket dredger, with buckets fastened to an endless chain – and powered it by three horses. The colliery was considered a modern marvel, and tradition has it that James I paid a visit in 1617. Unfortunately, no one had told the King that there were two shafts, one conventionally on land, and the second coming up on an artificial island on the foreshore. When the party emerged, the ever-suspicious monarch, finding himself surrounded by water, set up a loud cry of 'Treason!' and was not to be easily pacified again. But, however elaborate or ingenious the draining systems, they were never adequate to the job of lifting water from the deepest pits.

Conditions underground for the men, women, and children who worked in the early pits were always uncomfortable, frequently dangerous, and the work was invariably arduous. There were two main methods of winning the coal once mining had progressed beyond the crude bell-pit stage: the longwall or Shropshire method, in which the length of the seam was removed, the space being filled in by rubble to support the roof; and the pillar and stall method, in which only part of a seam was removed, thick blocks of coal being left behind to act as support. The tools that were used were the simple pick and shovel. Obstacles such as large rocks were at first dealt with by the crude but effective technique of fire setting. The fires were lit against the rock, and, when it was hot enough, cold water was thrown on, the sudden contraction causing the rock to split. Gunpowder did not come into use until early in the eighteenth century.

The job of hacking out the coal from the seam was arduous, and the job of hauling the coal along the narrow passages to the shaft and then to the surface was hardly less tiring. And very early in the history of mining the presence of dangerous gases was being noted – the explosive fire-damp or methane and the suffocating choke-damp or carbon dioxide. Dr Keys, the founder of Caius College, Cambridge, wrote in the mid sixteenth century: 'We also have in the northern parts of Britain certain coal pits, the unwholesome vapour whereof is so pernicious to the hired labourers, that it would immediately destroy them, if they did not get out of the way as soon as the flame of their lamps becomes blue, and is consumed.'

By the end of the seventeenth century, the coal trade was booming, especially in the north-east. Daniel Defoe visiting Tyneside in the 1720s looked in wonderment when he saw 'the prodigious heaps, I may say mountains, of coals, which are dug up at every pit, and how many of those pits there are; we are filled with equal wonder to consider where the people should live that can consume them'. The demand for coal was growing – wood was no longer the primary domestic fuel and new uses, such as in glass-making, were calling for greater stocks of the fuel. Improvements were introduced: above ground the first simple railways or tramways were built in the north-east to take coal from pit-head to port. At first the horse-drawn trams ran on wooden rails, one horse pulling four or five trucks. At the pit-head itself, the horse gin was introduced to wind men and materials up and down the shaft. This was a simple device in which a horse walking round a circular track turned a vertical drum round which a rope was wrapped, the other end passing via pulleys to the shaft. But underground, conditions were primitive and all attempts to go deeper were still frustrated by the problem of water. A technological breakthrough was needed if mining in Britain was not to reach a premature and watery grave. It came with one of the key inventions that formed the basis of the Industrial Revolution – the steam-engine.

The first step was taken when Captain Savery invented a 'fire engine'. The principle was not new: scientists had for a long time been investigating the properties of the vacuum, and were well aware that if a vacuum could be created then water could rush in to fill it, and the water could then be forced out again using hot air or steam. But theory was one thing and practice something quite different and Savery was the first to make a practical machine that used that theory. In his application for a Patent in 1698, he at once made it plain that he was very conscious of where his invention would prove most useful by heading the document 'The Miner's Friend' and attaching an address to 'The Gentlemen Adventurers in the Mines of England'. In this he wrote that 'For draining of mines and coal-pits, the use of the engine will sufficiently recommend itself in raising water so easie and cheap, and I do not doubt that in a few years it will be a means of making our mining trade, which is no small part of the wealth of this kingdome, double if not treble to what it now is.'

Savery was a little optimistic about the efficiency of his new invention, and if the men who had to work with it treated it with some suspicion, then they had good cause. Savery's engine worked underground, and an essential part of the process was the supply of high-pressure steam to push the water out of the cylinder and up towards the surface. Given the state of technology at the end of the seventeenth century, the danger of an underground boiler explosion must have been more a probability than a possibility.

The engine was both inefficient and dangerous but, as is so often the case, once a start had been made, improvements followed rapidly. In 1712, Thomas Newcomen built his first engine at a coal-mine near Dudley Castle in Staffordshire. The invention was credited jointly to Newcomen and Savery, but the latter's name appeared only because his original Patent had been so sweeping and general in application that almost any steam-engine design was covered by it. The Newcomen engine was an immense improvement over the Savery model. It was a beam-engine, and a monstrously huge device it must have seemed at its first appearance. From one end of the great wooden beam, pump rods were suspended by chains; from the other, a piston that moved in an open-topped cylinder. Steam was allowed into the cylinder and then condensed by jets of cold water, creating a partial vacuum. Air pressure forced the piston down, and at the other end of the beam the pump rods were raised. When pressure was equalized, the weight of the pump rods pulled the end of the beam down and the piston came up again, ready for the cycle to be repeated. The great beam rocked backwards and forwards, the pump rods worked steadily up and down in the shaft. The great advantage of the engine was that it used low-pressure steam, so that the boiler need be little more than a giant kettle and there was virtually no risk of explosion: in any case, because the rods pulled water upwards, it could be built at the surface instead of below ground. The disadvantage was that it was an inefficient machine in terms of fuel use, but for coal-mines where, by their very nature, fuel-supply was a minor problem, the Newcomen engine seemed less a man-made invention than a gift from the gods. It seemed that, at last, a new age of deep mining could begin and that the old enemy, water, had been conquered. New pits were sunk, old pits that were thought to be drowned out, reopened. Even the engine itself promised a new demand, for as the technology of the steam-engine developed, so the demand for fuel to feed the new machine grew. Hardly surprising then that more and more people began to see prospects of an Eldorado in the mineral wealth beneath the ground, as even the aristocrats joined in the hunt, tearing up their parks in the hopes of finding coal beneath meadow or wood.

The men who had to win the coal found less to cheer in the new technology. As the use of engines spread, the depth of the mines steadily increased and with the increasing depth came increasing danger. Even before their introduction, fire-damp had begun to claim its victims. The first of many tragic explosions occurred at Gateshead Colliery on Tyneside early in October 1705 when thirty people died. Three years later, on the Wear at Fatfield, there was an even more violent explosion. According to an early account 'the sudden eruption of violent fire discharging itself at the mouths of three pits, with as great a noise as the firing of cannon, or the loudest claps of thunder, and sixty-nine persons were instantly destroyed. Three of them, viz., two men and a woman, were blown quite up from the bottom of the shaft, 342 feet deep, into the air, and carried to a considerable distance from the mouth of the pit.' These were isolated incidents, but the sudden increase in the numbers and depths of pits brought a new regularity to the numbers of explosions.

The steps taken to fight fire-damp were crude and, because the real nature of the problem was not understood, ineffective. It was soon obvious enough that a naked flame would ignite the gas, but the solution to the problem of providing a working light without fire was not easily overcome. Many methods of lighting were tried: lights from the sparks of a steel-mill were thought to be safe, which they were not, and bizarre methods were tried such as using the luminescence of putrefying fish. It seems incredible that men could ever have tried to work in that absolute blackness with no more light than that faint glow, incredible too that they could have worked with the stench.

As the eighteenth century progressed, the dangers of the deep

30

mines were increased as gunpowder was introduced for blasting. One obvious solution to the fire-damp problem was to remove the gas before blasting. The unenviable task of dealing with it went to the fireman. He would cover himself in sackcloth soaked in water and crawl towards the gas. Once he was in place, he would lie flat on his stomach and light a candle which was then attached to a long pole. Then he would thrust the pole into the pocket of gas. The explosion would then pass over the body of the fireman, the damp sacking acting as a protection against burning. That, at any rate, was the theory. It was hardly an adequate answer to the problem of fire-damp, and in some pits the men either refused to go down or worked as best they could, fumbling in the dark.

Choke-damp too was a problem and it was soon evident that ventilation could provide an answer. In the old pits enough air found its way to the workings with no help from man, but in the deep pits something more was needed. The commonest method of ventilating was to set a furnace at the foot of a shaft. The hot air would rise up this upcast shaft, and fresh air would be sucked down a second downcast shaft to take its place. At first the air was simply allowed to pass along the face where work was actually in progress, allowing gas to gather in the wastes or old workings. Continuing explosions soon convinced colliery managers that the only solution was to ventilate the whole pit, so the galleries and roads were turned into a vast labyrinth, along the whole length of which the air was coursed by using a series of trapdoors to keep the air current in its right path. The system only worked if the doors were kept shut, except for the short time when men or wagons had to pass through. The job of looking after them fell to one of the most unhappily famous figures in mining history – the trapper boy. These young boys were given the job of crouching, alone, in the dark, hour after hour, opening and closing the doors to keep the fresh air flowing. The safety of the mines depended on these small children, but the nineteenth century was to be well on its way before most people in Britain even knew of their existence.

The new technology was pushing mines farther and farther beneath the surface of the earth, and the changes in mining techniques were dramatic enough for mining to share a part in that general movement we now call the Industrial Revolution. But for all the rapid changes in drainage and ventilation, relations between mine-owners and men were more medieval than modern. In Scotland, in particular, men spoke of the serfdom of the mines. They might more properly have spoken of slavery, for, in eighteenth-century Scottish mines, we can see oppression at its bleakest. The Scottish owners were as quick as their English counterparts to embrace the new technology, but in other areas they remained determinedly feudal.

The Scottish miner was governed by a unique law which decreed that he could not leave one mine to work in another without the consent of his employer. In theory, he could abandon mining for other work, but what work could he hope to find in a country already deep in poverty and made worse by the ravages of the '45 Uprising and its aftermath? In any case, the mining communities were isolated, apart from the rest of society, and the roofs over the miners' heads were there by courtesy of the mine-owners. So, in practice, the Scottish miner was tied for life to the mine he would first enter as a child, and if that mine changed hands then he and his family changed hands with it, carefully listed in the inventory like slaves or cattle. Had those miners had the time or the ability to read, how would they have responded to the accounts of manufacturers and other wealthy men of Britain and their campaign against the black slavery of America? Would they have grimaced at the irony or would they have followed the words of a later labour leader and adapted those comfortable gentlemen's toast of 'Success to the insurrection of the blacks' and cried out, 'Success to the insurrection of the whites'? By the end of the century, however, Parliament had removed the iniquitous law from the Statute Books. Nothing in the legislation, however, affected the atrocious conditions under which the Scottish miners laboured.

Robert Bald wrote a *General View of the Coal-Trade of Scotland* which was published in 1812 and which gives a vivid picture of the conditions in Scottish mines in the eighteenth century. Many of the incidents and working methods he describes were typical of all eighteenth-century mines, others, mercifully, were not. The first part of the work he describes certainly falls into the first category – the sinking of new pits. This job was alarmingly dangerous in the early days of gunpowder blasting. In sinking an engine pit, working among the flying dust from the blastings, the light from the candles stretched no farther than a few inches. Every hour the men had to lay a fine trail of powder to the main charge and then jump into the basket to be hauled as rapidly as possible away from danger. But, as Bald calmly remarks, 'it frequently happens that the train takes fire ere they have ascended a few fathoms; so that the splinters of stone fly around them in all directions; and the sound of the explosion is so overpowering, as to make the ears tingle, and suspend the sense of hearing for some minutes'. Yet the men who did this work might well have considered themselves fortunate when set beside those whose job it was to win the coal and carry it to the surface. It is easy to see why when one follows an account of a day's work for a mining family.

The men left for the pit late at night, usually at about eleven o'clock, taking with them any of their sons old enough to manage the work. As the rest of the world settled down for sleep, the miner began to hew the coal from the seam. Most of the Scottish coal was hard and the seams narrow. The work 'requires such constant exertion and twisting of the body, that, unless a person has been habituated to it from his earliest years, he cannot submit to the operation'. Bald noted some of the attitudes the miner had to adopt to get coals from different seams: lying full length in a 30-inch seam or sitting with body bent to one side. Some positions sound more like instructions for advanced yoga students than working methods, such as sitting with the right shoulder resting on the inside of the right knee, hacking away at coal at the level of the feet.

Some three hours after the men had gone, the women set out for the pit. Babies were wrapped in blankets and deposited with one of the old women who acted as baby-minders. The women's work was to take the cut coal from the face to the shaft or even 'to the hill' as the surface was known. In Scotland, when Bald wrote, there were four methods of moving the coal. In the most modern collieries, the coal was loaded into baskets which were dragged by ponies to the shaft, where machinery such as the horse gin or even a steam-winch could draw it to the surface. In others, the coals were carried in wheeled corves, or trucks pulled by women or boys to the shaft. But in very many pits, the coals were carried to the shaft on the backs of women bearers, and in the fourth and cruellest work method, the women had actually to carry the coals up ladders to the top of the shaft and then on again to the coal-heaps some distance from the pit-head.

The use of women bearers was unique to Scotland, and by the end of the eighteenth century it had been banned in the Glasgow region. Nevertheless, the practice was still widespread and Bald, who shared the growing preoccupation with quantitative studies took the trouble to calculate just how much work the unhappy women were forced to bear. Noting that it took two men to load the wicker-work basket on to the woman's back, he measured the load and found it a startling 170 lb. He then measured the distances the load had to be carried: from the face to the shaft was a steady uphill climb of 150 yards; from there she climbed by ladders 117 feet to the pit-head and then carried the load another 20 yards to the store. This journey she had to make at least 24 times a shift, working from 8 to 10 hours. A strong woman could shift, in this way, almost 2 tons of coal in a day, humping it for a horizontal distance of over 2 miles and vertically for nearly 3,000 feet. Small wonder then that Bald observed that 'it is no uncommon thing to see them, when ascending the pit, weeping most bitterly, from the excessive severity of the labour'. And for this they received the handsome payment of 8d. a day.

Even this is not the end of the catalogue of horrors that is the story of the women who worked in Scotland's mines. There were two classes: the wives and daughters of pitmen who worked within their own family group, and the fremit or framed bearers. The latter were attached to no particular miner, but were sent wherever the overman below ground chose to send them. They were powerless: if sent to an ill-tempered miner there was no redress against curses or even violence; if sent to a tyrant, then they were forced to bear whatever load the man chose to place on their backs, working on until either their spirits or their bodies broke. The last word on these poor wretches should go to

33

one of the women themselves. When she met Bald she was 'groaning under an excessive weight of coals, trembling in every nerve, and almost unable to keep her knees from sinking under her. On coming up, she said in a most plaintive and melancholy voice: "O Sir, this is sore, sore work. I wish to God that the first woman who tried to bear coals had broke her back, and none would have tried it again."'

At the end of a shift the family had the walk home to the cottage. They were still in their pit clothes and pit dirt, soaked with water, covered in mud and, in winter, their clothes all but froze stiff as they walked. Once home, there was no brightness, only the deserted house. The babies had to be collected and fed first before life could return slowly to the house. Such a way of life and such poverty had their inevitable consequences in disease and death. Among the young children in mining communities where the women worked, mortality was appalling; infectious diseases were rampant and the general poverty did nothing to help strengthen the resistance to epidemics. Bald noted many instances where death-rate exceeded birth-rate.

This was the blackest part of the Scottish mining scene. Where horses replaced women as bearers, the community underwent a transformation. The wife staying at home could make a home. The men and boys returned to a warm fire and a hot meal instead of cold and desolation. The home now became a place to be enjoyed, a place to be improved, a source of pride. Bald noted especially a love for grand imposing furniture – with a strong preference for mahogany. 'A chest of mahogany drawers, and an eight-day clock, with a mahogany case, are the great objects of their ambition.' The eight-day clock was the badge of success and when the trophy was finally won, neighbours and relations were invited in to stare and wonder and celebrate the great day. The same taste was shown in the north of England where John Holland in his book *Fossil Fuel* (1835) noted: 'Most of the old pit men had a taste for expensive furniture – a taste still indulged by many; and it would be impossible for a stranger to pass in front of the lowly dwellings, three or four hundred in number, adjacent to Jarrow Colliery, for example, without being struck by the succession of carved mahogany bed-posts, and tall chests-of-drawers, as well as chairs of the same costly material, which are presented at almost every open door.'

From Somerset to Clackmannan the pit villages held their poverty in common. There were the same huddles of mean buildings round the pit-head – a community certainly, but not a village or town in the accepted sense, more a makeshift colony. For the pitmen often seemed to be like colonists in a foreign land, apart from the rest of the country. They were drawn together by shared work, shared experience, and by the powerful ties of shared danger. Each coalfield had its own characteristics, but they were facile differences when set against the things they shared. But apart from the bleak face of the arduous work and poverty, they shared too in a love of gaudy. Not that there were many chances for bright display, but just as there was a pride in bright gleaming mahogany as a contrast with the black dust-filled air of the mine, so too when the chance came there was a rush into finery and bold display. Here is a description of a pitman's wedding:

'October 14, 1754. William Weatherburn, pitman, belonging to Heaton, was married at All Saints' Church, in Newcastle, to Elizabeth Oswald of Gallowgate. At the celebration of this marriage there was the greatest concourse of people ever known on a like occasion. There were five or six thousand at church and in the churchyard. The bride and bridegroom having invited their friends in the country, a great number attended them at church; and being mostly mounted double, or a man and a woman upon a horse, made a very grotesque appearance in their parade through the streets. The women and the horses were literally covered with ribbons.'

On these days, the pitmen of the north-east appeared in their best. Their hair was long and well brushed, hanging loose over their shoulders, where on working days it was kept in a pigtail or rolled into curls. On their heads they wore hats decorated with bands of brightly coloured ribbons into which they stuck bunches of small flowers such as primroses. Over their shirts they wore the brightest of all their clothes – the posey jacket. These were marvellously rich-coloured waistcoats embroidered with all kinds and varieties of patterns. The final splash of colour came with the stockings, dyed purple, blue, or pink or sometimes a mixture of colours. For a time at least the miner could get away from perpetual blackness.

Throughout the eighteenth century, the mining communities remained isolated and ignored by the rest of the country. Odd snippets of information have come down to us about their way of life – in Lancashire, for example, we learn that the miners had already started keeping racing pigeons, a pastime more harmless than that attributed to the miner by some of their contemporaries, who appeared to regard him much as a Roman might have regarded a Pict or Celt, as a species to be kept, by preference, behind a very high wall. The main difficulty in attempting to build up a picture is that one cannot apply a piece of information gleaned from one area to another area. The various districts had virtually no connections with other mining communities until well into the nineteenth century, and for many areas the information is scant indeed. But as that century came to an end, the miner began to appear more frequently in the public eye, the story becomes clearer, and a new phase of mining history began.

Chapter Three

The Two Wars

By the beginning of the nineteenth century, the miner's life was increasingly dominated by two great struggles: the fight for survival in the ever-more dangerous world of deep mines, and the fight against the coal-owners. The first was to prove the more deadly, the second the more bitter.

In the first struggle it is easy to cast a burgeoning technology in the role of villain. The Industrial Revolution was needing more and more coal: coal was in use for iron-smelting, so that where the ore and the fuel occurred close together in Shropshire, Staffordshire, and the rapidly developing centres of South Wales, there was a mining boom; the steam-engines ate up coal in prodigious quantities; the new industrial towns and villages all demanded more fuel. So coal-mining grew – more pits, deeper pits and, with an apparent inevitability, more dangerous pits. At the end of the seventeenth century, production had been running at nearly 3,000,000 tons a year; by the end of the eighteenth it had passed the 10,000,000 mark and was growing fast. Yet the technology that was forcing the pace, was easing some parts of the miners' burden as well. For, in truth, technology takes no sides – only men decide how and where it is to be used.

On the positive side, there was the complete abandonment of the system of carrying coals to the pit-head on human backs. The horse gin and the steam winding engine put an end to that. The pit-head began to take on its now familiar appearance, as the wheels span above shafts where men and coals were raised and lowered. Underground too there were great changes. In 1776, the mining engineer John Curr introduced the four-wheeled corve running on iron rails or plates to the underground workings. Instead of the putters, whose job it was to move the coal, having to manhandle their baskets of coal along the roadways, coals could be moved with much greater ease. Curr published details of his system in book form in 1797, and described how his corves could be pulled in trains of up to twelve by means of a horse gin. One horse, he reckoned, could shift as much as 150 tons a day along a 250-yard roadway. This was very evidently a much more efficient and more economical method of moving coal. It appealed to both colliery manager and colliery worker – a rare enough event. The view of the putter was expressed in a poem 'Pitman's Pay' by Thomas Wilson. The dialect, appropriately enough, is Tyneside:

> God bless the man wi' peace and plenty
> That first invented metal plates,
> Draw out his years te five times twenty,
> Then slide him through the heavenly gates.
>
> For if the human frame to spare
> Frae toil an' pain ayont conceevin',
> Hae aught te de wi' gettin' there,
> Aw think he mun gan' strite to heaven.

Note that change came quickly, and even in the most modern mines coal often had to be hauled along narrow, low passages before the plateway was reached.

Efforts were also made to improve ventilation. As pits became more and more complex and the galleries more extensive, so the old system of passing a current of air round all the workings became less effective. At the Walker Colliery in the north-east, for example, the air had a 30-mile journey from the downshaft to the up, at the end of which it must have been nearly as unbreathable as any of the other dangerous gases in the mine. A big difference was made when a system of compound ventilation was introduced, in which more than one current of air was used. But in spite of this the dangers of fiery mines in which men used gunpowder and naked flames continued to grow. The mine explosion from being a rarity became almost a commonplace. The bare statistics need little elaboration. Here are the figures quoted by the author Matthias Dunn for accidents in the Durham and Northumberland coalfield between 1790 and 1840:

	No. of accidents	Deaths
Explosions	87	1243
Suffocation by gases in the pit	4	18
Inundations from old workings	4	83
Falling of earth, rubbish, &c.	15	33
Chains or ropes breaking	19	45
Run over by trollies or waggons	13	12
Boilers bursting	5	34
	147	1468

Although explosions accounted for less than two-thirds of the accidents, they accounted for 90 per cent of the deaths. There had been mine explosions before these dates, but it was in the nineteenth century that the scale of accidents and the numbers of casualties increased dramatically. The public at large finally became aware of the problem in 1812 when an explosion, far worse than any previous explosion, caused the death of ninety-two workers at the Felling Colliery on Tyneside. A local clergyman, the Reverend John Hodgson, published his *Funeral Sermon* and, at last, steps were taken towards improving mine safety – tentative steps, less effective than seemed at first to be likely, but a beginning.

The explosion at Felling occurred at 11.30 on the morning of 25 May 1812, the early shift having just left and the next shift having just started. The colliery was considered very modern, with a furnace at the foot of one shaft, the William Pit, and steam-engine and horse gin at the top of the downshaft, the John Pit. Underground haulage was by wicker-work corves on plateways in the narrow roadways and in the main roadways by mechanical haulage. The shafts were over 600 feet deep and 550 yards apart. Felling may have been a deep pit, but it was considered a safe modern one. It made the great explosion seem all the more horrifying. The shock was felt as much as half a mile from the pit as, with a roar like artillery-fire, flame shot first from John Pit then, within moments travelled through the workings to shoot out in turn from William Pit. It was months before the bodies could be recovered: the ninety-first victim was brought out in the September, the ninety-second was never found.

The Reverend John Hodgson lived at Heworth, close to the pit, and it was his duty to perform the burial services for the victims. Little more was expected of him than that he should preach a sermon, say some words over the graves, and let the subject of mine accidents rest with the bones of the dead. But, to his very great credit, the Reverend Hodgson did a good deal more. He determined to publish an account of the accident in hopes of arousing public opinion to take action both to provide help for the victims' families and to provide some more permanent form of aid. The mine's owners, the very wealthy Brandling family of Gosforth, were horrified: the mine and what happened in it were of no concern to anyone but themselves and they vigorously opposed the publication. The Reverend Hodgson went ahead and published his *Funeral Sermon*. It contained plans of the workings, detailed lists of the dead – from which we learn that a third of those killed were under fifteen years of age – and a clear, full account of the explosion itself. Here is a small part of his description:

'Immense quantities of dust and small coal accompanied these blasts, and rose high into the air, in the form of an inverted cone. The heaviest part of the ejected matter, such as corves, pieces of wood, and small coal, fell near the pits; but the dust, borne away by a strong west wind, fell in a continual shower from the pit to the distance of a mile and a half. In the village of Heworth, it caused a darkness like that of early twilight, and covered the roads so thickly, that the footsteps of passengers were strongly imprinted on it.'

The language is unemotional, the reporting dry, precise, but the effect is perhaps all the greater. Men who had never given a thought to the subject were suddenly made quite vividly aware of the terrible effect and devastation of a colliery explosion. Where more emotional prose might have been more dramatic, the matter-of-fact, accurate description of events made it seem more real. The effect was achieved, working on a London barrister, J. J. Wilkinson, who travelled to the north-east and began agitating for the setting up of a society for the prevention of accidents in mines. The first meeting of the society was held on I October 1813.

As a direct result of the society's work, Sir Humphry Davy was brought to the north-east, where he began his experiments to determine the causes of mine explosions and to try to develop a safe working lamp. In November 1815, Sir Humphry read a paper to the Royal Society 'On the fire-damp of coal mines, and on methods of lighting the mines so as to prevent explosions.' By the end of the year he had produced a wire-gauze lamp, in which the fine gauze prevented the flame from causing an explosion in the gas outside the lamp. The lamp was the famous Davy safety-lamp. Simultaneously, but quite independently, George Stephenson produced his own safety-lamp design which was used for many years in the north-east. Theoretically, the appalling dangers of explosions in mines had been significantly reduced: in practice the opposite was to prove the case. The mining industry was to see catastrophes far worse than that at Felling, and more than a century of deadly explosions had to pass before the risk was really significantly reduced.

The fight for safety in the pits began with much good-will among all sections of the community: the same could not be said about the fight for decent wages and a civilized way of life for the miners. The period of the Industrial Revolution has been characterized as a period of rapacity and greed among employers. Like all such generalizations it must be treated warily and there were many exceptions in many different industries. But there were few enough exceptions in mining. The owners of Britain's mineral wealth were, in large part, the rich landowners and aristocrats under whose acres the coal was to be found. Some, such as the Duke of Bridgewater, who owned extensive mines at Worsley near Manchester and earned an entry in the history books as the promoter of Britain's first canal, threw themselves vigorously into the business of mine management. Many others, however, were content to draw substantial payments for the mineral rights and leave it to others to worry about the problems of winning the coal. In either case, the landowning classes had a very substantial interest in the mining industry. Where other classes of industrialists often had no direct voice in the unreformed Parliament before 1832, the mine-owners had. The interests of mine-owners were thus those of the ruling classes, and they tended to regard disputes between masters and men as a fight between established order and the forces of anarchy and revolution. The mine-owners had heard the stories of aristocratic heads tumbling into baskets before the guillotine, so to every demand for better pay and conditions, or even protest against pay cuts, they raised a howl of 'Jacobinism'. In such circumstances the conflict could hardly have been other than bitter.

In the early part of the eighteenth century, there was little or no organization among the mine-workers. Disputes between miners and employers, if not settled amicably, could easily flare into riot. There was no regular pattern to it. Attacks by the men were not limited to mines and mine buildings, as more than one publican in the ruins of his inn could testify. The end was inevitable: the magistrates read the Riot Act, the military moved in, and those thought to be the ring-leaders were arrested. Often it seemed that they were totally undirected eruptions of violence, as though the safety-valve had been screwed too tight on to a dangerously seething situation. The rest of the population – not perhaps surprisingly – began to fear the miners. They seldom saw or heard about the men who spent their lives under the earth except during the sudden outbreaks of rioting, and so came to regard them as a black and heathen tribe living among the civilized world but apart from it. The pattern began to change in 1765.

Each coalfield had its own customs and practices, and in the collieries of Tyne and Wear there was a system of hiring men on the Yearly Bond. Each autumn the owners and managers took on their work force for the following year. The men signed on for a nominal fee of 1s., though this could be increased in years when labour was scarce to as much as three guineas. This system did not mean that the men were guaranteed one year's work. On the contrary, the Bond placed no obligation on the owners to provide any work at all. It did, however, place an obligation on the worker to report for work whenever the owner required him. That in itself was bad enough, but in 1765 the owners brought out a new variation. They proposed that no miner should be signed on unless he produced a leaving certificate from his previous employer. Now, in effect, this would have reduced the north-eastern collier to the pitiful condition of slavery under which his Scottish counterpart suffered, since employers had only to refuse to give the certificate to ensure that the men were bound for as long as the employers deemed them useful. The men were not slow to see the implications of the new proposals. A few years earlier the result might have been sporadic outbursts of rioting and machine-breaking in the pits, but in that August the men acted with a surprising unanimity and struck work.

The strike of 1765 is an extraordinary early example of the power of concerted action by miners. Four thousand men came out and they stayed out. The authorities, conditioned by years of a familiar pattern in mining disputes, brought up no fewer than three troops of Dragoons and quartered them in the mining areas. The magistrates were ready with the Riot Act, but there were no riots. Instead the strike continued. Six weeks the men stayed out, until the owners capitulated. The leaving certificate disappeared from the Yearly Bond. It was a famous victory. The men, acting together, had preserved themselves from an iniquitous burden, but among the miners many abuses remained, of which the system of truck payment or the tommy shop were among the worst.

The truck system involved paying the men directly in goods in lieu of cash, but this was not as common as the tommy-shop system, where the men got their cash but were required to spend it at shops owned by the mine company. Many benevolent onlookers saw much virtue in the system. As they saw it, the kindly owner provided a house for his worker, gave him the benefit of a shop where he could buy all the necessities of life at a reasonable price and, at the end of the month when pay-day arrived, would even give him cash if there was any balance left to give. 'Thus', as the Society for Bettering the Condition of the Poor put it in 1798, 'the collier . . . is not able to squander the mass of his gains, to the injury of himself and his family.' Other observers were less convinced of the benevolence of a system that placed the employee at the complete mercy of the employer or the employer's agent. Employers argued, often with justice, that they provided goods at lower cost than the men could have obtained elsewhere. Employees could argue, with equal justice, that prices could just as easily be fixed high as low. The system was so obviously open to abuse, and so often abused, that in general it earned every word of condemnation that was applied to it.

The legislature clearly took a jaundiced view of truck. They were convinced by the argument that for an owner to set his own prices and then force his employee to pay those prices was indeed wrong. They were also aware of the justice of the argument that the tommy shop acted as an effective barrier to the employee leaving his job, since he was permanently in debt to the shop. The first anti-truck Act, which applied solely to the wool industry was passed in 1726, and from 1749 other anti-truck Acts followed. But the mine-owners were able to ensure that the mining industry was carefully excluded from all the legislation. Not that the legislature ignored the miners altogether nor excluded them from all their Acts. The miners got an Act of their own in 1800 which imposed harsh penalties on anyone damaging mines or mine property which 'are greatly exposed to the Depradations of wicked and evil-disposed Persons', and on anyone breaking their Bond. They were certainly not excluded when between 1799 and 1800 the famous, or infamous, Combination Laws were passed, which dealt a damaging blow to the growing power of the miners and the possibilities of co-operation.

The Combination Laws at least possessed the virtue of great simplicity: they made it illegal for any workman to join together with any other workman to demand more pay or shorter hours. Anyone who attempted to do so could be called in front of a magistrate – as like as not to be the employer with whom he was in dispute – and, if found guilty by his combined judge-prosecutor, could be sent to prison. The Act spread wide to include anyone supporting workmen who combined or attempted to combine – so wide in fact that anyone giving money for the defence of workmen charged under the Act was liable to find himself charged for his troubles, to stand in the dock in his turn. The Laws were rushed through Parliament by Peel, with no chance being given to the workmen to argue their case. The intention was clear enough – to smash any movement towards trade unionism before such a movement could become a powerful force in the land. On the simple equation of the rulers, workers such as miners were simply embryo Jacobins to be suppressed while suppression was still possible. Troops were moved into the manufacturing districts for all the world as though they were occupying forces in hostile territory. But, in one sense, the Acts failed – for they failed to convince working men that combination was not in their best interest.

The quarter century following the passing of the Combination Acts were violent and turbulent years in the mining industry. Wages gradually sank and men trudged the districts looking for higher pay. Whatever Parliament might say about combinations, there was no end to abuses in the industry, and men inevitably reacted against them. Denied the right of peaceful combination, what was there left to the men but the old style of riot and destruction? In South Wales, the coal industry was closely tied to the iron industry, and there were serious disturbances throughout the period. The largest employers were the Dowlais Company of Merthyr Tydfil, and they were absolute in their opposition to combination: an unfortunate workman who spoke up when the Company doubled the price of coal supplied to the workers' families, soon found himself in prison. From there he wrote: 'I ham sorry that I abuesed your Honer in taking so much Upon me to speak for Others. . . . Get me out of this whole of a place.' More seriously, there was a riot in 1800 against the introduction of a tommy shop.

In the next few years wages in South Wales fell, but in 1816 a move by the New Tredegar Company to lower them still further finally roused the men to the point of rebellion. They marched to Merthyr where they were joined by the men of Dowlais. Guest, the head of Dowlais, hurriedly signed up a band of special constables and armed them with pikes, but they were no match for the growing army of workmen and were easily disarmed. Guest himself

45

hurried back to his home, whence shots were fired into the crowd, injuring several workmen, one fatally. The men turned away but continued their procession round the ironworks and collieries, the columns growing ever larger until there were some 20,000 men involved. In near-panic, the authorities rushed the Glamorgan Regiment to the area, but the two sides never clashed. The masters and magistrates consulted, and at the end of their deliberations the notice of wage reduction was withdrawn. The jubilant men went back to work, but the unfortunate ring-leaders were fired. When they applied to the parish for poor relief, they were sent back to the parishes of their birth, safely out of the way.

In the north of England events followed no very definite pattern. It became common for the owners to use the Combination Laws as a big stick, taking out proceedings against the leaders of strikes and agitations, but withdrawing the accusation when the men publicly recanted. On one such occasion in Cheshire in 1811, where a group had met secretly to formulate wage demands, the leaders signed such a public apology, in which they had to 'humbly acknowledge the impropriety of our proceedings and return our thanks for the lenity we have experienced in the very serious prosecution that pended over us, being withdrawn'. Such public renunciations inevitably had a demoralizing effect on the mining communities, and worked strongly against combinations. Where strikes met the full force of the law, men turned instead to a more direct form of action.

At Radstock and Paulton in the Somerset coalfield, the men came out in February 1817 and, according to an account in the *Annual Register*, 'collected in a number of about three thousand and manifested some very serious symptoms of riot and destruction to the pits and the buildings annexed to them, which spread the greatest consternation through the whole neighbourhood'. The Riot Act was read, but the men continued, taking over pits and swearing not to return to work until their grievances were met. The following day, the men, armed with clubs, faced up to the cavalry, with shouts of 'Bread or Blood!' Inevitably, the cavalry won that skirmish, a number of men were arrested and, within days, the rest were back at work. The account ends with a little homily to the workers to 'avoid those blasphemous and seditious publications which have caused their riotous conduct', and recommends them to 'look to their masters as their best friends'. It also mentions, in passing, that the best friends had just reduced wages by 10 per cent. That the miners themselves never felt altogether benevolent towards the owners had been graphically demonstrated the year before when, in a riot at Dudley in Staffordshire, they had put a noose round the neck of an owner, Zephaniah Parker, and threatened to hang him if he did not agree to their demands.

Stories of riots are very common at this time but, in spite of the laws, the miners still managed to band together in the north-east for the great 'Binding Strike' of 1810. In 1809, the owners decided to change the date of the annual binding from October to January. The men felt that this put them at a disadvantage, having to bargain in the coldest part of the year when work was scarce and prices high. When the binding day arrived, men from the different mines met at Long Benton and a strike was called. The delegates toured the various districts throughout the strike to help preserve unity, but all the time they were hounded by the owner-magistrates. Durham Gaol was filled to overflowing, and the Bishop of Durham charitably loaned his stables as a temporary prison. Nearly 300 men were herded in there guarded at first by the Durham Volunteers and later, when the authorities decided they could not trust local men for the duty, by the Royal Carmarthenshire Militia. Miners have long memories: a vicar whose parish included a pit village wrote, in 1862, that he had visited a miner's house only to be accosted by the miner who accused him of speaking against the Union and who ended the encounter by 'taking the knife that he was using for the purpose of eating his food, and striking it menacingly, he expressed a vehement wish that he could stick it into the Bishop of Durham'. However, for all the combined efforts of Church and State, the miners held out and after seven weeks the owners capitulated. A new binding date was fixed for April and new terms drawn up under the supervision of a local magistrate, the Reverend W. Nesfield. The lesson for the future was plain.

The repeal of the Combination Laws in 1824 and 1825 was like a signal-rocket. Trade Unions suddenly appeared where, for a quarter of a century, none were supposed to have existed. What happened in those years is partly hidden by the secrecy imposed on the men who were threatened by the law, but it is obvious that the organizations did exist, sometimes as clandestine organizations, meeting in secret with all the paraphernalia of oath-taking and ceremonial, or disguised as friendly or benevolent societies, existing only to collect money for sick funds or accident payments. Unions were now lawful, but that made them no more acceptable to the powerful owners. The real struggle between mine-workers and mine-owners could now begin in earnest.

Working the Mines

Many early mines were drift mines, cut into a hillside, a type of which this independent mine in the Forest of Dean is a rare survivor.

Most mines were, and are, reached by a vertical shaft and shaft sinking was one of the most hazardous jobs facing the miner. The illustration of 1878 shows men descending down a partly lined shaft.

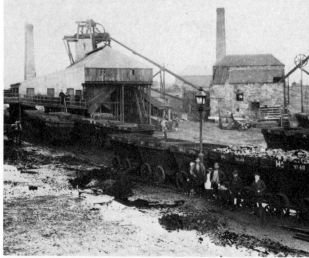

Above: Sinkers, in their distinctive clothing, coming up the new shaft at Wallsend in the 1890s. Top right: Modern sinking presents a different prospect with precast concrete sleeves being lowered into place at Rothes Colliery, Fife. Centre, below: Above the shaft, the pit-head scene scarcely changed through the nineteenth and well into the twentieth centuries. It was dominated by the engine-house of the steam-engines and their accompanying headstock gear.

Above: As fresh shafts were sunk, so fresh headstock gear was added.

Left: The modern skyline has changed dramatically: Bevercotes Colliery.

Right: The life of the miner has changed, but much remains the same. He still fills his water-bottle before descending into the dusty pit.

In wet mines, the miner
still greases his boots to keep
the water out.

The working day begins with
the queue for the cage at
Monk Bretton Colliery,
Doncaster. Below: In many pits,
there was a long and, for the
uninitiated, back-breaking
walk to the face.

Modern transport improvements include this odd 'ski-lift' transport at Clifton Colliery, Notts.

The comparative luxury of a train ride at Bwllfa Colliery, Aberdare.

Below: Work at the face in the days before mechanization could involve men in labouring in almost impossible conditions in narrow seams.

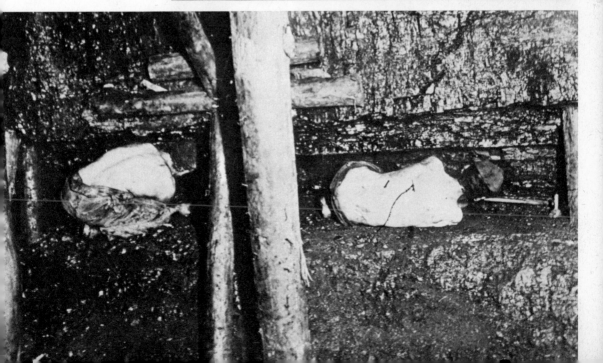

Above: Men contorted themselves into strange yoga-like positions to reach the coal. Below: In the wider seams, work was more comfortable, though it is interesting to note that in this photograph (right) taken in 1919, a candle is used for light.

Left: In higher seams a man might kneel. Right: The lucky miner could stand at his work, but the work was hardly less exhausting. Below: In some mines the workers had the worst of all worlds. Condering Colliery is now closed, but the photograph shows what happens when a low seam combined with a wet pit to produce truly appalling conditions.

Drilling into the face before blasting, as here at Ashington in 1911, was another arduous job.

Even the introduction of power drills brought little relief.

The holes drilled, the blaster rammed the charge home.

Top: Machine-cutting was introduced as early as the nineteenth century. The hydraulically powered cutter was pictured in this engraving of 1867.

Above left: There were many technical difficulties to overcome – and much reluctance to invest capital in new equipment – so that scenes such as this were rare in the early twentieth century.

Above right: Today's colliery, such as Dobson Main, has powered cutters and loaders, and hydraulic props that move forward as the face moves forward.

Left: Behind the hewers were the loaders who man-handled the coal into waiting trucks, as here at Cannock Chase in the 1920s.

Above left: Some worked on their knees, shovelling the hewn coal, as at Wetmess, Fife.
Above right: Once the job of moving the coal to the shaft fell to women and children, later
to men. Below left: Some release from man-handling came with the introduction of horses
and ponies. The engraving shows a European mine, Creuzot, where the horse is being
lowered to work. Below right: The pit-pony had a long history in British mines. Here,
looking like some prehistoric monster, he draws men to work.

Many ponies lived
their lives in
underground stables.

Boys often
tended the ponies.

When the ponies did emerge, the filth and damp in which they often worked could be seen in the wet, matted coat.

In the modern pit, the work of man and beast has been given to the conveyor, as at Whitehill Colliery.

Above left: The underground train. Above right: Supervision old style, by the traditional deputy at his checking point.

The underground worker goes down and stays down for the length of his shift. He takes his 'snap' down and gets few interruptions and fewer visitors.

The control room and closed-circuit television of Bevercotes.

King George V and Queen Mary were clearly planning no trip
to the coal-face in their visit to Silverwood in 1912.

The Prince of Wales went underground at Cwmner in 1919.

Above: Screening the coal was a job that often went to older workers or men who were too ill to go down the mine. This curious scene at St Hilda in 1901 looks more like work at one of H.M. Prisons with the overseer literally overseeing.

Left: Women often worked on the screens, like these women at Haydock in 1948.
Right: Today, machines have taken over screening.

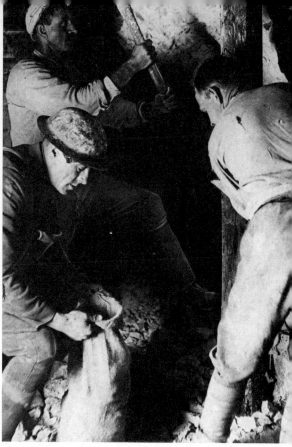

Left: Not all coal is gained underground. Open-cast mines such as this have little in common with the traditional pits. Right: If coal was not always underground, so the underground worker was not always winning coal. In the First World War many miners found new employment as sappers. Below: For many, coal was always there for the gathering on the beaches of the north-east, washed ashore from coasters. This crowded shore is at Seaton Carew.

Chapter Four

The First Unions

The various mining districts moved towards Unionism at different speeds. The Scots appear to have been first off the mark in 1824. A pamphlet published in that year, *Address to the Colliers of Ayrshire*, began by celebrating the fact that 'the remains of Gothic barbarism and feudal tyranny, known by the name of Combination Laws, have been swept from the Statute Book'. It continued by giving an account of a miners' meeting at Kilmarnock, when delegates from twenty-seven pits met and decided that 'it would be highly expedient to associate for the general good of the trade'. The new Union was soon in conflict, when more than a thousand Ayrshire miners came out on strike and stayed out for two months.

Unionism in the north-east got off to a very unpromising start. A co-operative was formed at Hetton in Durham by a miner called Mackintosh, but he was accused of having his fingers in the till and made a hasty exodus for America. In 1830, another Hetton miner led a Union with, at first, considerably more success and always with considerably more honesty. The miner was Thomas Hepburn and the union became known as 'Hepburn's Union'. Like the Scots, the men at once began to show their militancy. On 12 March 1830, there was a great meeting on Town Moor, Newcastle, at which 20,000 workers from Northumberland and Durham turned out. The meeting was peaceful, but the demands firm. The most important points included the reduction of hours for boys down the pit to twelve per day and drastic alterations in the tommy-shop system. The next month the demands were sent to the owners. Some points were agreed, but the owners found the men in no mood for compromise – it was to be all or nothing. The strike began.

Once begun, it soon appeared that there was in fact very little unity among the men, and many went back to work. Those who remained reacted violently and pits were forcibly closed, often with the destruction of machinery. One small incident says a good deal about the mood of the men. A large group of them broke into the house of the notably unpopular overseer of Cowpen Colliery. They ransacked his larder and emptied his cellar, but left the house, furniture, and occupants unharmed. The overseer got this letter the next day:

'... I see ye hev a greet lot of rooms, and big cellars, and plenty wine and beer in them, which I got me share on. Noo I naw some at wor colliery that has three or fower lads and lasses, and they live on won room not half as gude as your cellar. I don't pretend to naw very much, but I naw there shudnt be that much difference ... ye maisters and owners may luk out, for yer not gan to get se much o yer awn way, wer gan to hev some o wars now.'

The authorities reacted strongly. Special constables were sworn in, the local Militia marched to the mining districts, and a detachment of Marines was shipped out from Portsmouth. The area was one huge armed camp, with soldiers at every pit and cavalry patrols at night. There was violence on both sides and everything seemed set for a long and bloody struggle when, quite suddenly, in the middle of July, the owners capitulated.

The men saw it as a triumph and a short time afterwards appointed Hepburn as a full-time, paid Union official. The celebrations were premature. The next year's binding saw the start of a new campaign. This time the owners refused to sign on Union members and the inevitable strike began. If the previous year's struggle had been fierce and bitter it was nothing compared to that of 1832; this time the owners' aim was simple, to smash Unionism in the north-east. They brought new tactics to bear. Now the owners realized the value of the cottages they owned and rented out to the miners and their families. They began to import labourers from other parts of the country, usually at very low wages, and to evict their old employees to make way for the new men. Violence was bound to follow. More special constables were sworn in and given the job of eviction, and they were also empowered to arrest any miners collecting in groups. Given arbitrary powers, the constables acted in an arbitrary manner. Serious trouble erupted at the Friar's Goose Collieries, where the police were stoned by miners. But, as so often in the past, the combined powers of owners, police, and military proved the stronger, and backed by the new policies of eviction and importation of blackleg labour, they were all but irresistible. Slowly the move back to work began as men left the Union. The battle was lost, but the violence was by no means ended.

On 11 June, Nicholas Fairless, a local magistrate, was dragged from his horse and so savagely beaten that he died from his injuries. William Jobling, a miner, was tried for the murder, convicted, hanged, and his body was hung in chains from the gibbet. On 8 July there was a second death. There was a scuffle between strikers and police – a common enough occurrence – but on this occasion one of the miners, Cuthbert Skipsey, tried to intervene to restore order. A constable, George Waddle, drew his pistol and shot Skipsey dead. Waddle too was tried and convicted, and sentenced to six months' hard labour.

The strike never really ended, it simply petered out. The Union was broken and Hepburn was broken with it. The men he had led were forced to renounce the Union, while he himself was driven to beggary. Eventually he was forced to walk the coalfields looking for work and accept the final humiliation of promising to take no further part in Union activity. He was then taken on at Felling, where he worked out his days in a miserable anonymity.

In South Wales, too, events were gathering a new momentum. The fight against truck and tommy shop had begun in earnest in 1829. Even local magistrates, not noted for their fervent support of working-class causes, warned the Home Office of the dangers of allowing the truck system to go unchecked: 'Great as certainly is the pressure of the times upon the labouring classes, your petitioner is thoroughly convinced that the distress arising therefrom is grievously endangered by the pernicious practice, which of late has too generally again obtained of masters paying their workmen in goods instead of in money.' He could well have been right, for there was certainly a growing feeling of resentment and a growing solidarity among the men, who agreed to support men on strike by paying out cash from a common fund. This was a major step forward for the workers, and effectively prevented the owners from introducing piecemeal wage reductions.

Nevertheless, the main issues in South Wales remained unresolved. In June 1830, the men held a mass meeting at Merthyr to discuss strike action. Thomas Guest of Dowlais pausing briefly to exchange his employer's hat for his sheriff's hat, arrived with troops and began reading the Riot Act. To his deep chagrin, the men took matters into their own hands: they attacked the soldiers, disarmed them, and sent them scampering off for safety. For a week at least the workers ruled in South Wales. But it could not last. The soldiers returned in force, the disorganized movement collapsed, and the leader Dick Penderyn was hanged.

The immediate danger over, the masters began taking an interest in the development of organized Unions in the north-east of England. Thomas Guest heard from a correspondent that the miners 'had some cause of complaint' in 1831, but now they 'do as they like'. He and the other employers determined to stamp on Unionism before it could begin to grow and flourish. That year, the Welsh miners tried to form a Union, only to be faced by a demand from the employers that they should sign an agreement not to join. After a three months' strike the men gave way, and the employers sat down to consider ways in which they could consolidate their position. An ingenious plan was put forward of issuing discharge papers, so that any man leaving a colliery would have to carry a document saying why he was leaving. Men sacked for Union work could thus be kept permanently out of work or taken back only when sufficiently humbled. Thomas Guest also tried the power of argument in a pamphlet addressed to his workmen. He warned of the evils of Unionism and put forward the novel doctrine that mine-owners shared with popes and Charles I the advantages of Divine appointment: 'In providing for your own house,' he sternly admonished, 'you are not to infringe on the providential order of God, by invading the rights of others, by attempting to force upon those whom God has set over you, the adoption of such regulations and the payment of such wages as would be beneficial to yourselves.'

Unions or no Unions, the real grievances and complaints of the Welsh miners were not to be wished away by pamphlets and speeches. The Union Clubs became first semi-secret, then, in the face of continued harassment of Union members, they went underground. The secret organizations found their own methods of combating the employers' techniques – as common in Wales as elsewhere – of eviction and the employment of blackleg labour. If the employers insisted on bringing in blacklegs, then the miners were prepared to drive them out again. A new, strange name appeared in the valleys – 'Scotch Cattle'. It was a secret organization that soon made it quite plain that it was prepared to use violence to obtain its ends. Early in 1832, menacing signs – bulls' heads, painted in red to simulate blood – appeared on the doors of blackleg labourers employed by the Nantyglo Company. The following night, the houses were attacked, furniture broken, and many of the men beaten. Foot-soldiers and cavalry were sent to search out the raiders. Reward notices were posted offering £15 – a fortune to a working man – to anyone giving information. Rival notices also appeared, written in the usual threatening red, denouncing 'traitors and turncoats' and threatening to pull out the hearts of such men, and to fix two hearts on the horns of the bull. No information was given: the society remained secret, and the members formulated the demands that might otherwise have been put forward by a less violent body had the Unions not been suppressed. A local newspaper deplored the movement, but had to admit its effectiveness.

'We have to record further acts of outrage and violence perpetrated by those nocturnal yclept "Scotch Cattle". On Wednesday last week, about 200 of these deluded men visited Blaencwm Colliery, distant from Pontypool about three miles, and commenced in their usual manner, destroying furniture, etc., of the colliers and otherwise injuring the houses by hurling immense stones at them. They have, unfortunately, succeeded in intimidating the peaceable and well-disposed from pursuing their labour. There are scarcely any collieries in the hills that have escaped their visitation, the most of which have been stopped working. It seems that the men are determined to be paid weekly for their labour in the coin of the realm, and will not be compelled, as before, to deal in the shops of their employers.'

The bands of men, faces blackened, brought terror to many nights in the valleys. For a time nothing would be heard of the Cattle, but when disputes arose and the old story of eviction and blacklegging was repeated, then the Bulls would roar again. As late as 1843, during a particularly hard struggle which saw many of the miners' leaders in gaol, the Cattle were active. When the men of Rosca Colliery decided to return to work, they received due warning that the Bull was coming. 'Unless you comply with our terms we will show you the worth of your lives you Rosca fools, you are all working under the drop.' On this occasion the techniques of eviction and imprisonment succeeded and the strikers were defeated; but it demonstrated, as did the earlier incidents, that where lawful protest against genuine grievances was suppressed, the only inevitable answer was unlawful and violent protest. The ironmasters and mine-owners were the true begetters of the Scotch Cattle.

Throughout the 1830s there seemed always to be agitation at hand in one coalfield or another. In 1837 it was Scotland's turn with a fierce conflict centred on the Lanarkshire mines. The men there had begun to restrict the hours of the darg, or day work, while the owners showed their determination to resist any shortening of the working day. The owners were well placed, for in this area were many many families in a condition of desperate poverty, notably the hand-loom weavers whose livelihood had been steadily eroded by the introduction of power-looms. They, and gangs of Irish labourers, were brought to the pits. The new recruits were protected day and night, marched to the pit under guard, and guarded again in their homes when they returned. Their lives were the lives of convicts, and they lived surrounded by the hostility and hatred of their neighbours. It is perhaps a measure of the wretchedness of their condition that such a life seemed preferable to what they had known before. The strike lasted for months, during which time there was much violence, but in the end the men capitulated and Unionism in Scotland was temporarily broken.

Towards the end of the 1830s a new voice was heard that helped to foment conflict in the coalfields – the voice of Chartism. But the attempts of the Chartists to nominate August 1839 as a 'sacred month' or, more prosaically to call a one-month general strike, ended in fiasco. At the end of the decade the miners' organizations were fragmented and purely local. In some regions, Unions rose only to be squashed again. The owners could use the lack of unity between the different regions to move trade round the country – where production fell in one area, it could be increased in another. Strikers were financially vulnerable, there were no central funds to help men on strike, and there were grave threats to be faced of eviction and permanent loss of home and job. It took a brave man – indeed, a brave family – to face the prospect of suddenly finding themselves forced into the gutter, their possessions, their furniture, thrown after them to scatter in the mud and dirt. The owners had the power of their own association, and beyond that they could call on the full might of the State to support them against the men.

71

But power can only suppress. The lives of the miners were made no better because their voices were not heard: the condition of their work and the condition of their lives were not changed by the presence of troops of cavalry and platoons of constables. As long as the grievances remained, then so long would the men continue to find a way to right them. And those grievances were real enough, as the country as a whole was horrified to learn in the 1840s.

Chapter Five
Men, Women and Children

It would not be unfair to say that most people in Britain in 1840 knew about as much of the life and conditions of the miners as they did of tribes in Central Africa. Occasional forays were made into the mining districts by those indefatigable and ever-curious gentlemen, the British tourists, but in general even they preferred areas where the news was not constantly of strike and riot. A few accounts of visits to working mines did reach the presses, but the mines visited were usually the most modern with wide, high roadways and underground tramways. The Reverend John Hodgson describes such a visit in his *Picture of Newcastle upon Tyne* published in 1807. The colliery he visited was East Kenton, which was connected to the Tyne by a tunnel three miles long. A single-line railway for horse-drawn trams had been laid, and the tunnel was roomy enough, some 6 foot high by 6 foot wide, to allow for sections of double track for trams to pass. From the description, a mine visit was a jolly jaunt, a pleasant outing to which even the ladies might safely be invited. Then, as now, visitors tended to be shown only the best: the writer described his tramway trip in glowing terms, describing how they paused at the sections of double track while the horse-boy called and listened for any approaching trucks and then how they waited for the loaded train to appear. He ends with a fine piece of romanticism: 'The candle of the boy coming down appears like a star in the distance, through the gloom, and has a very pleasing effect, as it gradually approaches.' He is scrupulous in pointing out that this system is unique to this particular colliery, but the account is not matched by any description of a more typical mine.

So the public remained largely in ignorance until, between 1841 and 1843, the Reports of the Royal Commission on the Employment of Children in Mines appeared. The ignorance was rudely dispelled, and the depth of the ignorance made the sudden revelation all the more shocking. It was the illustrations, more even than the words, the interviews, and descriptions, that made an immense impact. Here were portrayed men and women and small children living the life of beasts: a teenage girl struggling on all fours harnessed to a wagon of coal that she was pulling along a narrow seam;

75

little children clinging to a rope as they were lowered down a shaft by an old woman whose rags told of her poverty; boys chained to heavy corves, with only a single candle to light the dark roadways. The scenes were of wretchedness and poverty, of crue'' hard labour being borne in conditions of terrible discomf‾   ‾ing children. The pictures also produced a sense of m‾   ‾e sight of boys and girls, men and women wc‾ naked except for a few tattered rags. Fr‾ contemporary sources we have a ‾ down Britain's mines just ove‾

In the early nineteent‾ workers were haul‾ put their legs thr‾ raised or lowered ‾ historian of the coal ‾ younger boys thought recount a hair-raising e‾ 600 feet down a shaft, his ‾ rope was hauled back up ‾ This alarmingly dangerous m‾ introduction of cages by T. Y. ‾ the worker, but much more eff‾ Rails were set into the bottom of ‾ be wheeled straight in. But, at the ‾   ‾on, cages were still a novelty and travell‾   ‾al.

If riding the ropes down the shaft co‾   ‾ as fine fun, there was little enough in the pit itself ‾   ‾ earn the same title. The first thing anyone would noti‾ would be that total, velvety blackness, which the dim light of the Davy lamp seemed scarcely to penetrate. One of the factors that tended to diminish the benefits of the Davy lamp was its poor light: many miners, not understanding the principle, either tampered with the gauze or resorted again to candles in order to get a stronger working light. The next thing that would be brought to uncomfortable conscious-ness would be the heat and stuffiness of many of the deep mines. At Jarrow Colliery on a coolish day in 1820 the following temperatures were recorded: at the surface 46 °F, at the bottom of the pit, 876 feet down, 61 °F, and at the end of its journey the air tempera-ture was up to 75 °F. But the hottest place to be was the boiler-room of the engine-house where a temperature of 144 °F was recorded.

In the dark, hot passages, underground figures would be seen moving about, many of them naked or nearly so. The journey to the coal-face was usually acutely uncomfortable, as the miners had to bend low or even crawl in low places for many miles. Once at the face, the conditions to be found had hardly changed since the previous century. Certain 'improvements' had been made, such as the introduction of gunpowder for blasting. Though this greatly increased the efficiency of winning the coal, blasting brought a

76

dangerous increase in the level of dust in the mine and its own very obvious dangers. Engels wrote at some length in his book *The Condition of the Working Class in England* of the effects of coal-dust on miners. He described the disease known then as 'black spittle', caused by breathing in the dust. It 'manifests itself in general debility, headache, oppression of the chest, and thick, black mucous expectoration'. In some areas the disease was mild, in others, especially in Scotland, it was fatal. The more advanced symptoms were wheezing, short breath, a rapid pulse, and loss of weight. The black spittle was and is the great scourge of the mining districts, and though today we can give it the more scientific name of pneumosilicosis, we have not eradicated it.

Blasting did little or nothing to lessen the hard physical labour of the men who cut the coal from the seam or loaded it into the corves. There the amount of labour depended on the geology of the coalfield: where the seams were narrow, the men were still forced to contort themselves to win and load. In some mines the physical conditions were made even worse by the presence of water, turning the floors of the passageways into filthy morasses. Rheumatism was a common complaint of men in the wet mines. Put them together – lung disease, the strain of hard work in confined spaces, rheumatism, and you have an equation with an obvious solution – death. As Engels put it: 'in all districts *without exception*, the coal-miners age early and become unfit for work soon after the fortieth year, though this is different in different places. A coal-miner who can follow his calling after the 45th or 50th year is a very great rarity indeed.'

To us, today, such facts and statistics might seem shocking but they would have hardly made a great stir in nineteenth-century Britain. There were many occupations as likely to end in fatality – the grinders of Sheffield or Redditch could look forward to no longer life than the miners before they succumbed to chest disease; the lead-glazers of the Potteries needed to spend little time at their trade before the symptoms of poisoning appeared. These were known facts, established in the evidence of Parliamentary Committees, but the authorities showed little concern. Metal tools and needles needed to be sharpened, there was a demand for lead-glazed pots. It was unfortunate that the production of such commodities proved so lethal to the producers but it was, alas, inevitable. So, too, coal was needed, and if men must suffer to provide it then that was the way Providence had ordered affairs and there was nothing to be done. Yet the story of the women and children of the mines struck more sympathetic ears. Here was a situation that was felt not to be inevitable. Here was a bestiality not to be tolerated.

It was the use of children to move the coal from the face to the shaft that caused most of the outraged cries in Parliament and elsewhere in the country. In one mine, near Chesterfield, boys had to pull corves weighing at least $\frac{1}{2}$ ton and sometimes as heavy as 1 ton, for 60 yards along a roadway that was only 2 feet high. Where the roof was higher, asses could be used for haulage, and when the tramway was reached the corves were put on to the tracks: on a down gradient they could run under their own weight, but in other parts they were pulled by a boy with a 'dog belt' round his hips which was attached by chains to the corve. In some mines the haulier was helped by a second boy, pushing behind with his head against the truck. The conditions were particularly bad for the children in the Midlands coalfields where the organization of work was the responsibility of butties. These were contractors who agreed with the mine-owners to produce coal at a fixed price. Galloway considered that the name 'butty' might be a corruption of 'brother', but there was little enough that was fraternal about most Midlands butties. Their object was to lower production costs as far as possible below the fixed price to ensure maximum profits, and the easiest way to do this was to keep wages low or, in the case of children, extract as much work as possible. The boys who worked as hauliers might work as many as fourteen hours a day, from six in the morning to eight at night, and on top of that they would have an often lengthy journey to and from work. The pages of the Royal Commission Reports are full of accounts of children returning home too tired to eat, who fell asleep as soon as they sat at table and had to be carried to bed. Some were not even able to walk the distance to their homes, and parents would find them asleep by the roadside. It is a commonplace to speak of Sunday as 'a day of rest', but for the mine children the phrase had a real and deep significance, since it was only by staying in bed throughout their Sundays that they were able to summon up enough strength for the week ahead. The effects of such a life need no elaboration: they used to say you could tell a miner by his underdeveloped and twisted frame, and it would be little surprise if that were the case. This was the norm for the mining areas, but under the butty system the norm was often passed. The butties were notorious for their ill-treatment of the boys – working them on into the night, arbitrarily reducing their 'snap time' or meal breaks. As a body, with too few exceptions, the butties came second only to the blacklegs in the abhorrence in which they were held by the majority of the mining community.

The youngest children had what one must call the lightest work. They were the trapper boys, whose job it was to open and close the trapdoors that sealed off the roadways and kept the air passing along its appointed track. Hour after hour these little children sat by themselves in the dark, opening the doors for men and corves to pass, closing them again when they had gone. In later years, the attitude towards these children was to be quite sentimental, as in a poem published in the paper, the *British Miner* in October 1862. which begins:

Beside the ventilating door,
The little Trapper lay,
And sleep had clos'd his weary eyes,
As night shuts out the day.
He left his home before the sun
Had filled the earth with joy,
And to the pit did bend his way –
An English Trapper Boy.

But at first there was no sentimentality, and the danger to the whole mine of a trapper boy falling asleep was a real one. In any case, sentimentality was not an attitude commonly found among the owners, and it was a luxury that the families themselves could not afford. With low wages and a working life unlikely to stretch far beyond the age of forty, miners could not survive without the wages of the children.

Victorian society was clearly moved by the stories of harsh labour among the children, but they were profoundly shocked by the prospect of wholesale immorality underground. There was a thrill of horror as they considered the prospect of men and women working together naked in the dark places under the earth. As Engels noted: 'The number of illegitimate children is here disproportionately large, and indicates what goes on among the half-savage population below ground.' The response to the Report was immediate. Lord Ashley rushed a Bill into Parliament which banned all work by women underground and limited the hours that could be worked by children. The Bill became law in August 1842. The country settled down again, content that justice had been done and a great wrong removed. Unfortunately, as there was virtually no provision for enforcing the law, its effectiveness was sadly limited. Nevertheless, a principle had been laid down, a first step had been taken.

The Report was concerned with working conditions for a section of the underground work force, rather than with mine safety, but for all underground workers the dangers were increasing all the time. Traditionally, the pits of the north-east were regarded as fiery, but as more and more deep pits were sunk in other areas, so the number of fiery pits increased. In Lancashire, the pits in the Newton, Wigan, and Ashton areas were becoming explosive, as were some in the West Riding of Yorkshire. The Midlands were still comparatively free of fire-damp, and South Wales was still mostly engaged in shallow workings. Not that an absence of fire-damp meant that mining was safe, for there were many other ways in which the life of a miner was put in peril – inundation, roof falls, choke-damp, and more. Nevertheless it was death from explosion that gave most cause for alarm. Statistics for the early nineteenth century are scattered and incomplete, but enough is known to give at least a glimpse into the dangers of the pit.

The 1841 Census listed nearly 120,000 as coal-miners, a figure which helps to give perspective to the accident statistics. There was no official listing of accidents, though an attempt was made for certain regions to list the lives lost in the quarter century up to 1834. Unfortunately the figure did not include those for Scotland, Northumberland, and Durham. Nevertheless, incomplete as they are, they are frightening enough – 343 killed in the West Riding, 135 in Lancashire (though, here, not all districts reported), 104 in one district of Stafford, and 140 in Cumberland. Altogether, there were 954 killed in the period. The figure quoted in Fyne's classic *The Miners of Northumberland and Durham* are still more startling. Between 1756 and 1805 there were 44 explosions with the loss of 432 lives, but in the next forty years the number of explosions had risen to 75 while the death toll had soared to 1,270.

To gauge the mounting horror of pit explosions, one can perhaps get the clearest picture by studying just one notably fiery pit in the north-east – Wallsend Colliery. Between 1782 and 1820, there were 9 separate explosions and altogether 43 lives were lost. Then a shaft was sunk to the deep Bensham seam, 200 feet below the main seam and approximately 900 feet below the surface. The gas here was so prevalent that it could be used to light the pit: the men had only to drill a hole in the seam, stick in a tin pipe, seal it round with clay, and apply a light to the end of the pipe – instant gas-lighting. Men had always to be on hand after shot-firing to beat out the inevitable fires with wet sacks. In the main seam, a pair of cannon were kept on hand to blow out any fires that could not be doused by the men. Their presence could hardly have been an aid to confidence. In any case, local inhabitants had a constant reminder that this was, in the words of the famous mining engineer John Buddle, a 'prodigiously fiery' mine. Gas was brought to the surface at the C pit through a 4-inch iron pipe. It came out with a force that was said to produce a roar like a blast-furnace and burned with a flame that could rise as high as 9 feet. In October 1821, one year after sinking down to the Bensham seam, there was an explosion that 'shook the ground like an earthquake, and made the furniture dance in the neighbouring houses'. There were 56 down the pit – 4 survived. The ventilation at Wallsend was improved, with three downcast and two upcast shafts, but the flow of air was still sluggish and the pit a potential danger. That danger became a reality in June 1835. It was two o'clock in the afternoon and many of the hewers had just finished their shift, leaving the putters and hauliers to move the coal, and the trappers were at their posts. Some 90 men were back at the surface when there was an explosion. It did not seem, at first, to be very serious. The bankman at the top of G pit was just about to send an empty corve down the shaft when a great gust of wind blew it out again and carried his hat high above the headstock gear. Then there was a little light smoke, followed almost at once by silence. There was none of the dramatic earthquake effect of 1821. When the rescuers finished their task, they found that 2 furnacemen had escaped, 4 were alive at the foot of G pit, though one of these later died from his injuries, but of the remaining 101 in the mine, there were no survivors. Some had died in the fire of the explosion, the rest, scrambling to get clear, had fallen to the deadly after-damp, the carbon monoxide that formed after the explosion. The Wallsend disaster was particularly poignant, for so many of the victims – well over half – were young boys.

If the picture of life in the mines in the early years of Victoria's reign seems to be one of unremitting hard work for all the members of the workers' families, of dreadful conditions, of the real danger of death, either quick, by accident or slow, by one of the miners' diseases, then it must be said that that picture is very largely accurate. To that grim scene must be added the many abuses to which the miners were subjected. The men were often paid piece rates, but rates calculated in a very special way. For example, the coal would be screened and only the large coal retained on the screens counted towards the final reckoning. Did that mean that the small coal was simply worthless rubbish? Not a bit of it. Small coal was commonly used in the boilers of steam-engines, often at the very collieries where payment was refused. Again, the miners were subjected to a system of fines for offences, such as sending up corves not completely filled, so that a man might sweat over a corve, only to be told it was not officially full and lose the whole value of it. Some abuses were theoretically ended. The truck system had been finally declared illegal for the mining industry in 1831, but the enforcement of the law left a good deal to be desired. In certain areas, notably South Wales, one can only charitably assume that news of the legislation never reached the ears of either mine-owners or magistrates, though they appeared to have little enough problem with communications on matters more in line with what they took to be their own interests.

How was it possible in a reputedly civilized land for such a large body of the population to be systematically abused and oppressed with no apparent response from the rest of the community? In part the answer lies with the almost total isolation of the majority of miners from the rest of the population. In an interesting little book published in 1862, *Life among the Colliers*, an anonymous author describes how she married a mine-owner and went to live in a mining village. Friends sent messages of sympathy rather as if she had been a missionary embarking on a tour of duty among the head-hunters. The picture of life in the mining villages at that time is fragmentary, and scarcely received more documentation than did the head-hunters – and often information came in the same highly coloured and dramatic style. The accounts we have can roughly be divided into two categories: those, like an account by an 'Incumbent in the Diocese of Durham', which relate only the evil done by the miners, and those, such as that of the Socialist Engels, which relate only the evil done to them. Yet from the various bits and pieces some sort of picture does emerge, and it is fascinating to discover just what a strange, often exotic culture the miners retained.

The majority of descriptions of pit villages tell the same story of a huddle of cottages scattered round the pit and usually belonging to the pit's owner. In Scotland and the north-east of England, single-storey cottages were common, where elsewhere two-storey cottages were found. The 'Incumbent' described his Durham village as 'a dark, dreary, dirty, smoky hole', but notes that the houses were 'well ventilated'. From other accounts it appears that the good ventilation was caused by the wind that blew in the front door that opened on to the living-room/kitchen and blew straight out the back. The general pattern of two-storey housing was for one or sometimes two small rooms to be provided on the ground floor, with garret rooms, open to the roof, above. Deal planks laid over joists acted as both floor and ceiling, dividing the two levels. Where there were two rooms on the ground floor the cottages were rather grandly known as 'double houses', the second room acting as the main bedroom.

Conditions varied greatly between one area and the next and from village to village. An editorial in the *British Miner* of 1862 complained of the dirt: 'The conditions of many of the dwellings is most filthy: none of them have any direct water supply, and the drainage of the dwellings is almost entirely superficial: it is difficult to conceive anything more horribly offensive than the rears of some of the houses, where yards are filled with filth.' On the other hand, a guide to Durham County, published in 1834, describes the miners' terraces as having small gardens 'where they pay so much attention to the cultivation of flowers, that they frequently bear away prizes at floral exhibitions': interesting that the tradition of growing prize flowers and vegetables is as strong in the Durham mining community today as it was in the 1830s. In general, however, the story is more one of filth and squalor than of neat gardens. The condition of a village depended to some extent on the whim, or rather conscience, of the owner. Some terraces still remain as evidence of careful building and good maintenance – the worst have, in the nature of things, long since fallen down. Not that the good intentions of the owner were always appreciated. 'The Master', whose activities are described in *Life among the Colliers*, met stern resistance when he attempted such novelties as filling in the open sewer and laying a pavement in the village street to replace the footpaths of trampled coal-dust. Tidying up a village included 'splashing' the cottages – covering the walls with a kind of stucco-like mud.

This same authoress showed a lively interest in her new neigh-bours, and while finding some of their customs strange, she still found the miners to be very different from the savages she had expected. The odd hours worked by the hewers, three in the morn-ing to three in the afternoon, meant that they were around the village in the afternoon and evening. The first sight she got of them confirmed her fears, as they 'loosed out' from work; they looked, she said 'a rough set, a colony of sweeps'. For the journey to and from work, they wore, and insisted on wearing, jackets made of a wildly impractical white flannel. She noted that drunkenness was common but, unlike many of her contemporaries, does not labour the point, preferring to look at other aspects. She started a choir, which was a great success, although she never quite got the ascendancy over the independent-minded men, who would work with great enthusiasm at music that suited their tastes, but simply packed up and went home if it did not. Music had a special importance in the lives of many miners, and the church organist, after a full day down the pit, would then walk eight miles for a music lesson.

The book is full of small details about life and customs in the small Midlands village. The club system was very strongly entrenched – for example everyone contributed 1s. a week to the boot club, and then took it in turns to get new boots. Some events in the village had very special importance. Funerals were occasions of great ceremonial. They began with a long procession led by a powerfully singing choir and ended with funeral cakes being handed out to all neighbours and friends – to overlook anyone was an appalling social error. Christmas too had its ceremonials. King Coal, a huge block of coal decorated with evergreens, was carried in procession round the village. More, however, than all the strange customs or special rituals, it was the comradeship of the miners that most impressed the writer, the willingness of all to rush to the aid of any who suffered. If she had gone to a different village, she might well have found the customs as different as if she had gone to another country, but that comradeship at least she would have found the same.

Different areas meant different customs. In Durham, the men were paid fortnightly and, as many writers noted, pay-days were not marked by any great display of sobriety. But pay-days were also the time when the families did all their shopping, and the roads converging on the local market-towns were full of miners and their families. The area also had its own special Christmas customs, when the miners from the villages collected in Sunderland or Durham to perform their sword dances. The men wore white shirts covered with multi-coloured ribbons and were under the command of a Captain, dressed in cocked hat and faded uniform. The collecting-box was taken round by a clown or 'Bessy' who wore a fur hat with a dangling fox-tail.

Other customs and practices had rather less charm. All forms of gambling were popular among miners and drunkenness was widespread. Some local pastimes were quite startlingly violent. The following exchange, recorded in the 1842 Report on Child Employment describes the popularity of fighting in Lancashire.

'The colliers are great fighters and wrestlers. On Christmas day I saw twelve pitch battles with colliers.

'Were they stand up fights? – No; it is all up and down fighting here. They fight quite naked excepting their clogs. When one has the other down on the ground, he first endeavours to choke him by squeezing his throat, then he kicks him on the head with his clogs. Sometimes they are very severely injured; that man you saw today with a piece out of his shoulder is a great fighter.'

Violence was no stranger to the entertainments of the ordinary men of Britain a century and more ago – prize-fighting, wrestling, cock-fighting were all popular. As with other customs, the popularity of different entertainments varied from region to region. Certain characteristics seem to recur – a love of music and colourful ceremonial, but the differences are more marked than the similarities. It was the same diversity among the miners of different areas that made it comparatively easy for mine-owners to play off one region against the next. But, as the nineteenth century approached its half-way mark, the miners of Britain began slowly to realize that diversity meant weakness. 'Strength through unity' is today something of a cliché – then it was a battle-cry.

Away Home

Previous page: Lancashire men and boys come up from the day shift in 1920. Above: If the men were lucky, they might have a changing-room or even a pit-head bath. This early bath building, where the clothes hang like flags from the ceiling, was at Ellington, Northumberland. Left: For most, on pay-day, it was collect your cash then away home.

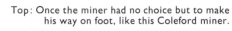

NOTICE
NO LOAD
EXCEEDING 12 TONS
TO PASS OVER BRIDGE
BY ORDER

Top: Once the miner had no choice but to make his way on foot, like this Coleford miner.

Centre: Today, there are easier ways for the miner to get home.

Right: Many collieries lay on their own special bus services.

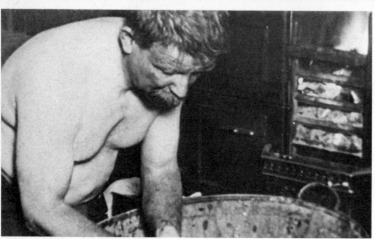

The pit-head bath is something
of a modern innovation. Until
quite recently, removing pit
dirt meant a tub before the
fire at home.

These rather spartan baths at Atherton were no doubt considered a great luxury in 1919.

Today, the showers are accepted as normal.

The men who came home from the pits too often returned to grim terraces with few amenities – privies at the bottom of the garden and spoil heaps for scenery.

This bleak square at Featherstone, photographed in 1926, was all too typical.

The miner's home was dominated by his job. Here the wife warms his pit clothes ready for a night shift in 1946.

Chapter Six
The Search for Unity

The cause of Unionism in the mines had suffered a major setback in the 1830s – not by any means its last – but surged forward again with new power in the 1840s. The country-wide agitation of the Chartists, though not successful in achieving its specific aims, did help in rousing the fighting blood of many of the working people of Britain. More importantly for the miners, Chartism made them aware that they had common cause that stretched beyond parochial boundaries. New Unions appeared, loosely based on county organizations, and there began a movement towards uniting in a national body. The Mining Association of Great Britain was formed at a meeting in Wakefield, Yorkshire, in 1841.

The Association was formed at first from the County Unions of the north of England, but the leaders proved themselves avid propagandists for their cause. Branches were soon formed in Staffordshire and Nottingham, where Unionism had previously been virtually unknown, and Scottish miners also began to take a prominent part in the proceedings. In 1844 the Association sent a message to the coal-owners requesting a meeting to discuss a new pay agreement. There was no reply from the owners, who quite simply refused to acknowledge the existence of the Union. On 25 March of that year there was a great conference at Glasgow, with delegates representing 70,000 miners. There was bitter resentment against the owners and their contemptuous attitude: delegate after delegate got up to air his grievances. Some told of systems of fines imposed for breaking rules it was impossible to keep, ending with a story from Tyne Main of a miner who 'worked for 1s 6d and there was 2s kept off him; so that he laboured all day for nothing, and had to pay the masters 6d for allowing him to do so'. So the tales of grievances rolled in, until at the end a resolution was passed agreeing that the miners of Northumberland and Durham should present the list to the masters on 5 April when they were due to sign the annual bond, and if they were not met they would strike. The delegates pledged themselves 'to do all in our power to assist them in their struggle, and also prevent men coming in amongst them'.

The bond day arrived and the men sent in their list of grievances. The masters refused to see the deputation and, at a vast open-air meeting, strike action was agreed. Every pit in the two counties was closed. There was a real unity of purpose, born in part at least of near desperation, for over the years the men had been unable to resist successive cuts in pay. Now they were acting together and were eager to have their case heard. In May they made a public recital of their wrongs. They catalogued the grim conditions of the mines, the bad air and long hours, the unjust system of fines, the payment by measure where the measures were set by the masters, supervised by the masters and, if there was any dispute, arbitrated upon by the masters. They told of young children in the mines, of pay reductions, and they stressed the injustice of the annual bond which said a man must report for work or be guilty of a crime, but that the master had no responsibility to give him work when he did come. The voice of the miner was heard loud and very plain.

The course of the strike followed a now familiar pattern of blacklegging, eviction, and military forces spread through the region. One new element was the savage vindictiveness of the important mine-owner, the Marquess of Londonderry, who, infuriated by 'his' tradesmen in 'his' town of Seaham allowing credit to strikers, sent this stern missive:

'Lord Londonderry again warns all the shopkeepers and trades-men in his town of Seaham that if they will give credit to pitmen who hold off work, and continue in the Union, such men will be marked by his agents and overmen, and will never be employed in his collieries again, and the shopkeepers may be assured that they will never have any custom or dealings with them from Lord London-derry's large concerns that he can in any manner prevent. . . . Because it is neither fair, just or equitable that the resident traders in his own town should combine and assist the infatuated workmen or pitmen in prolonging their own miseries by continuing an insane strike, and an unjust and senseless warfare against their proprietors and masters.'

His Lordship's cause and that of his fellow mine-owners was helped on its way by the magistrates who closed the workhouse doors against the strikers' families, leaving them to beg or starve.

At the end of July, almost four months after the start of the strike, another great meeting was held to demonstrate the solidarity of the strikers. A procession, with banners flying, marched through Gateshead and Newcastle to Town Moor. It was a brave show, and there were brave legends on the bright banners:

'Stand firm to your Union,
Brave sons of the mine,
And we'll conquer the tyrants
Of Tees, Wear and Tyne.'

It was a brave show, but only thinly disguised the marks of defeat. The Union was neither wide enough nor strong enough to support the strikers and, in August, after twenty weeks, the strike ended. It appeared to be a complete victory for the owners, but it later transpired that it had in fact written *finis* to the system of the yearly bond.

The repercussions of the 1842 strike were felt for a long time in Northumberland and Durham. The talk of unity had not been enough to stop the recruitment of Welsh miners to work during the strike, but once the strike was over the locals soon made known how they felt about those who had helped to break them. On 15 August, two local miners got into a fight with two Welshmen, and before long the fight had become a battle between two small armies. Garden fences were pulled up, pickaxe-handles collected – anything that would make a weapon was taken up by men on both sides. From four men, the numbers swelled to tens, and then to hundreds. Slowly, the Welshmen gave way before the angry crowd, retreating to the comparative safety of their homes, and only the arrival of the military prevented the mob from storming the houses. Ten of the local men were arrested, handcuffed together, and taken under armed escort to Shields.

It was not the violent riot, but the continual harassment of the Welsh, day after day, above ground and below, that finally demoralized them. Often the harassment could be cruel, affecting the weakest members of the community, the children. A common practice was to take away their candles, leaving the small boys alone and frightened in the absolute darkness of the mine. In defence of the locals, it must be remembered that many of them were still living in fields and by the roadside while the Welsh occupied their old homes. The Welsh left and the local families returned to their houses. Most found no difficulty in getting their old jobs back: only the strike leaders remained unemployed. But the strike had fatally weakened the young Mining Association, and support dwindled and then died.

Before its death, the Association had shown its vigour. It was a crusading body, sending delegates down to other regions to spread the message of Unionism. They had a good deal of success in raising membership in the Midlands. The area was soon engulfed in a whole series of strikes at various pits, against truck and against many of the evils of the butty system. The owners retaliated by lock-outs of Union men. The north-eastern story was repeated and again the Union crashed to defeat. But, just as in the north-east where the strike produced the first great crack in the bond system, so in the Midlands the attack on butties and truck was vigorously launched. The first battle was lost, but the war was just begun.

There were other positive gains made by the Unions in the 1840s, of which one of the most important was the gain of the backing of the law. In the past, the law had been seen as an implacable opponent of the miners, just one more powerful weapon in the coal-owners' armoury. Now the miners turned the weapon and began using it against the owners. The Northumberland and Durham miners brought in a solicitor, William Roberts, who was sympathetic to the cause of the Unions, to argue on behalf of the members in the courts. Before Roberts appeared, the miner was virtually power-less – often illiterate, invariably ignorant of the niceties and nuances of legal language, he was the inevitable loser in the endless quarrels over contracts, terms of employment, or in the many other disputes that ended up in the courts. Roberts brought a dramatic change to the scene. As successes mounted, he was given a permanent post by the Mining Association as their legal adviser at a salary of £1,000 a year. He also earned for himself the unofficial title of 'the miners' attorney-general'.

Roberts himself described his struggles to obtain justice for the miners in an article published in 1851 and quoted at length in the Webbs' *History of Trade Unionism*. He wrote of the strong pre-judices of the magistrates:

'It never happened to me to meet a magistrate who considered that an agreement between masters not to employ any particular "troublesome fellow" was an unlawful act; reverse the case, how-ever, and it immediately becomes a formidable conspiracy, which must be put down by the strong arm of the law, etc. . . . When I was acting for the Colliers' Union in the North we resisted every individual act of oppression, even in cases where we were sure of losing; and the result was that in a short time there was no oppres-sion to resist. For it is to be observed that oppression like that we are speaking of – which is after all a more genteel and cowardly form of thieving – shrinks at once from a determined and decided opposition.'

In 1844, Roberts was also instrumental in ensuring the defeat of a Bill that would have made it possible for a single magistrate, on the complaint of an employer, to issue a warrant for a workman's arrest and then imprison him.

Engels gives glowing accounts of Roberts's success, claiming that he had only to appear in a district for abuses to suddenly vanish. He quotes an example from Belper in Derbyshire where the 'attorney-general's' visit caused such flutterings among the owners that the following notice was at once posted:

'NOTICE

Pentrich Coal-Mine

The Messrs. Haslam think it necessary, in order to prevent all mistakes, to announce that all persons employed in their col-liery will receive their wages wholly in cash, and may expend them when and as they choose to do. If they purchase goods in the shops of Messrs. Haslam they will receive them as heretofore at wholesale prices, but they are not expected to make their purchases there, and work and wages will be continued as usual whether purchases are made in these shops or elsewhere.'

However, once Roberts was on his way, the fluttering died down again and the anxious pigeons and doves resumed their more normal hawkish appearance. One man could only do so much, and the economic crisis of 1847–48 saw the end of a period of decline for the Association and its total collapse. For a decade, Unionism in the mines was dead.

The story of the regrowth of Unions is discontinuous, each area moving in its own way at its own speed. But it was no longer quite the fragmentation of the early days. Men were conscious of the need for concerted action: local Pit Unions grew into County Unions, County Unions into national bodies. New leaders appeared, men such as Alexander McDonald who came down from Airdrie eventually to become the first President of the Miners' National Union in 1863. McDonald was the epitome of a new self-confidence: starting in the pits at the age of eight in 1829, he was able to educate himself so that by the age of twenty-five he could take a place at Glasgow University, keeping himself by working down the mines in vacation time. A pugnacious, loud, and rumbustious character he added force of personality to education and money obtained from successful speculation. He emerged as undisputed leader of the British miners.

Unionism was active again. The Fife miners listened to all the talk and agitation over the eight-hour day, decided talk alone was going to get them nothing and stayed down the pit until the eight-hour day was reality and not a dream. The event has a special place in the history of mines and miners, and every year the Miners' Gala celebrates the event.

As the County Unions grew, so they split into two large associations: the western counties of England joined with South Wales to form the militant Amalgamated Association of Miners in 1869: the older Miners' National Union concentrated on working to alter the legislation that affected the mines. That movement gained extra momentum, following the extension of the franchise, when McDonald and the General Secretary of the Northumberland Miners' Union were elected to Westminster, the first in what was to prove a strong and steady line of men who came from pit to Parliament.

Two features marked the miners and their organizations in the last part of the nineteenth century: there was a new sense of unity and interdependence, and a new eloquence and ability to make their views heard. The illiterate, disorganized mob, driven only by its own desperation and emotions, was giving way to an organized body, determined steadily and systematically to reduce and eliminate the abuses under which the whole mining community still suffered. A mark of this new power of the miner to articulate his feelings was the appearance of newpapers such as the British Miner which was first published in September 1862. It gave the individual miners from all over Britain an opportunity to make themselves heard. To read through the pages of this paper is to receive a vivid impression of the miners' fight for a decent living and a decent life. It is a disorganized picture, a kaleidoscope, but each fragment, though small, is highly coloured and adds to the brilliant pattern of the whole. The following extracts will perhaps give some idea of the attitudes of the men, who could now make their voices heard in print as well as in deed.

In the first editorial the paper proclaimed its aims. It was 'devoted to the interests of the working miners of the United Kingdom'. The general tone of the paper tended to be moral, improving, and moderate. The objective was to publicize the dangers of mining – 1,109 killed in 1862 – and to promote the British Miners' Benefit Association. They also affirmed that, in recording each mining disaster, 'it will be our further duty to trace, if possible, its cause, and, in case of wilful neglect, to assert the claims of the aggrieved to redress'. On the improving side they promised articles 'relating to Social Economy' and 'pages will inculcate morality and a due observance of religious duties'. They added that they would 'urge upon our readers to prefer the Savings Bank to the Beer House'. Although they went on to press for legislation to improve the miner's life, they were generally opposed to strikes, which they tended to regard as the work of dangerous outside agitators and charlatans: 'Only the other day, a would-be *leader* – an ignorant pill maker – *modestly* asked £200 a year, to be paid out of the pockets of the toiling, industrious colliers, in consequence of *his very valuable* (we say very questionable) *services* . . . we maintain that a strike for wages is never, in the long run, attended with success.' Such was the tone of the first editorial – the voice of moderate Victorian reform. But in the news items, and especially in the many letters to the Editor, a quite different voice soon made itself heard.

The working miner was quick to grasp the opportunity to make his views public – and two themes soon emerged, butties and truck. Many butties practised the 'drinking system'. At its most blatant, this consisted of the butty or overseer starting a drink club into which all men were compelled to pay a part of their wages. In return, the men were supplied with a ration of beer by the butty, in quantities determined by the butty, and at a price set by the butty. If not legally definable as robbery it was precious close to it. Many butties kept beer-shops at which men were forced to spend money or risk losing their jobs. The truck letters were as numerous as the butty letters, and they named names. A letter in the issue of 31 January 1863 refers to James Merry, a mine-owner and Member of Parliament, as 'the great truck king of Scotland'. He employed about a thousand men in his mines and ironworks and paid them monthly. As the men never caught up with their pay, they were forced to accept advances. Merry was quite prepared to advance money, with just the one proviso – all the money had to be spent in the Company's shop. That was the worst, but not the only, abuse at Merry's. There were regular stoppages from pay: 2d. a week for the doctor, 2d. for the school – money was even stopped to pay for the blacksmith who sharpened work tools. There were stoppages for house rent. The families were thoughtfully provided with coal for a stoppage of 4s. a month – and received not very much less for the money than if they had gone to any coal-merchant in the district. Such was the story of a truck system organized by a Member of Parliament in a country where truck was illegal. There were many more stories in similar vein.

Although the paper was officially opposed to strikes, it opened its correspondence columns to strikers who often explained their case with great lucidity. Typical of the accounts of smaller strikes was one of a strike at Methley Junction Colliery, where the system of payment for coal was arbitrarily changed. Previously the men had received 1s. 1d. per ton, but with only two days' notice given, they were ordered to sort it into big and small pieces, 'which is putting a deal of extra work on the men', and the rate was altered so that they got 1s. 3d. for large coal (an increase of 2d.) and 9d. for small (a decrease of 4d.). To add to their problems, the colliery already only paid in 5 cwt measures, rounding down, need one say, and never up, so that a man bringing 19 cwt to bank received cash for only 15 cwt. The writer records that in one week when they had only one day at work, they lost 10 ton 2 cwt by this rounding down. With work irregular, a deputation went to ask for a higher rate that would put them on the same rates as near-by colliers. 'All the answer we got was that he (our master) made his own laws and we must go by them, he had nothing to do with our neighbours.' The writer ends: 'It has been rumoured that we are sullen and stupid, and will not go and talk with our masters; but we have been and we have told you of our reception.'

Other letters amplified the themes. A writer from Barnsley pointed to the contempt in which men were held by the owners who sacked miners who questioned commands, issuing them with 'tickets of leave', giving the reason for dismissal as 'not sufficiently subservient'. There were more stories of the abuses of the payment by weight system. At some pits, coals had to be pressed down to completely fill the tubs and if, as often happened, in their long journey from face to pit-head the coals settled down farther, the bankmen could classify them as not full and refuse any payment. So a man could sweat all day in a 3-foot seam and see no reward for his labours. At other collieries, the coal was screened to calculate payments – the screens known to the owners as 'Billy Fair Play' were ironically christened by the men 'Billy One Side'.

There were also stories of the men fighting back. In Fife, owners were prosecuted for using inaccurate measures – a steel-yard, for example, was found to underweigh by 12½ per cent. There were calls for support for strikers, for financial aid for men such as the 40,000 Scottish miners locked out in 1863. The men had refused to take a 10 per cent wage cut and the gates were shut against them.

'The last act of petty tyranny is to be played. The well-fed coal masters now drive what was but a few days ago their workmen, and from whose toil, sweat and blood, they derived their luxuries and comfort, with his wife and family, to the street. These Christians have agreed to starve the hungry, uncover the poor, and leave them homeless wanderers.'

This is the true, clear voice of the oppressed just as this voice is the new voice of militancy: 'Miners of Wigan, Ince, and other parts of Lancashire, you could once hold up your heads, and could ask for your just rights without fear. The truth is at present you are abject slaves, for the want of a hearty Union between yourselves.... Union is your only safeguard.'

Whatever the *British Miner* might have set out to be, its readers ensured that it became a voice for action. Mine-owners clearly had no doubt on that point, and a new item of May 1863 described the eviction of two miners and their families for selling it. One of them, William Edwards, had a child that was dangerously ill but that did not prevent their being thrown into the street. It was expected that the child would die, for no one dared take it in.

The pages of the paper are not all taken up with complaints and conflict. Each week there was a fiction serial, and there were many accounts of self-improvement, such as a letter from Dudley describing how the miners had a reading-room and had formed a 'mutual-improvement class'. There were speeches and debates. The subjects for discussion at least had the virtue of breadth, for after 'a social tea party' they planned to discuss 'the principles of capital punishment and popular amusement &c.' – a daunting combination. This type of item was greatly favoured by the paper, and reflected the influence of Methodism in so many of the mining districts. But for all that, it was the familiar story of conflict to which the paper most often returned. It is interesting to compare the accounts of industrial action with the accounts that appeared in the other great mining paper, the *Colliery Guardian*.

The *Guardian* was the paper of the mining engineers, and took a firmly management line. When the voice of the miner appears – not a common occurrence – it is a selected voice. In the issue of 27 March 1858, for example, there are a number of reports of industrial action in Yorkshire. The men were protesting against reductions in pay of 15 per cent, and the masters had responded by attempts at intimidation. One of the strikers, William Moorhead of the Waterloo Pit, was charged with leaving work without giving one month's notice and sentenced to a month's hard labour. The paper also quotes, with evident approval, a letter from a Yorkshire miner opposing the strike. He hopefully writes that 'if we act with care and caution, and go about the business in a proper and legitimate way, we may persuade our masters not to be so hard on us'. Such views did not find their way to the pages of the *British Miner*. Every issue had its stories of strike and conflict. To get a complete picture of the industrial battle waged in the coalfields of Britain would involve an almost endless list of individual campaigns, but perhaps the feeling of the age can be gauged by a close look at one big group of strikes – those of the Welsh miners between 1871 and 1875.

Already by 1871, the Amalgamated Association of Miners had made enormous progress in South Wales. Local lodges had been formed in all the mining districts, and a central organization with its own funds was well established. As with so many disputes, the story of the strikes is complicated by the extraordinary complexity of organizations and interests that characterized the industry in the nineteenth century. Just as groups of miners formed local unions and later amalgamated into wider associations, so the owners acted individually and in their own associations. In South Wales the owners could be grouped into three categories: the Ironmasters' Association, the Steam Coal Colliers' Association and a multitude of interests known simply by the negative title of 'non-Association'. Not surprisingly they found some difficulty in agreeing to any united action.

The first moves came in February 1871 when all groups announced a 10 per cent cut in wages, but before the battle could be joined the Ironmasters suddenly announced that they had changed their mind and would only impose a 5 per cent reduction. With bad grace, the other two groups fell into line. Having won the first battle without a shot being fired, the men pressed their advantage. On 1 May they put in a demand for a 10 per cent increase and again found the enemy divided. The Ironmasters and some non-Association pits very soon wavered and offered a 5 per cent increase. This was accepted. But this time the Steam Coal Colliers' Association decided to continue the fight on their own, and on 1 June the strike began. This strike is particularly interesting for it is well documented, including a very full account of the owners' position by their leader Alexander Dalziel which he published in 1872.

The strike began on a now-familiar course. The aim of the owners was simple enough – to break the new and rapidly developing Union. Dalziel records that at a meeting of colliery managers at Aberdare on 12 May, a resolution was passed which stated that 'unless the proprietors resist to the utmost any demands of the men for an advance of wages at the present time, it will be impossible to manage them'. This, Dalziel says, was more important than 'the mere monetary consideration'. The owners called in the notorious strike-breaker Paul Roper to recruit 300 men and boys to work in the pits, and they agreed to pay 6s. for every workman he could bring to Aberdare and the Rhondda. The main recruitment drive was in Staffordshire and Cornwall, but the unsavoury Roper, who even Dalziel speaks of with contempt, did not have an easy passage. The new unity of the Association of Miners was brought into play, and the Staffordshire men did their best to deter workers from going into Wales. In a message to the Welsh strikers they averred: 'Respectable men will not come into South Wales; nothing but the very scum of the country will put their feet upon your soil . . . stand firm. *Don't be downhearted.* We will stop all we possibly can.'

Handbills and posters were distributed in Staffordshire.

'MINERS!

The bill of Paul Roper, stating that 500 men are wanted is
ALL DECEPTION. They are only wanted for a few weeks
in South Wales, where 9000 men have been on strike for
eight weeks. Miners of South Staffordshire! Stay at home,
and the South Wales miners' case is sure.'

Inevitably workers did come into South Wales and, equally
inevitably, could only work and live under the constant protection
of the police. The authorities by this time were so nervous of the
growing self-confidence of the men, that instead of calling on the
local Militia, they actually disarmed them, for they could no longer
be certain on whose behalf they would use their weapons. But, in
spite of the protection, more and more of the imported labourers
succumbed to the lectures and cajoling of the strikers and began to
leave the district. By mid August there was not a blackleg at work
in South Wales. With their most powerful weapon slipped from
their hands, the owners agreed to meet the miners and then agreed
with them to send the case to arbitration. The men went back
to work and, after a good deal of procrastination, the arbitration
agreement was published. The men were given an immediate $2\frac{1}{2}$
per cent increase with a further rise of 10 per cent in the following
May and it was agreed that, in future, rates would be tied to those
paid by the Ironmasters.

The men had won but they had little enough time to savour the
victory. At the end of 1872, the owners announced a 10 per cent
cut in wages. The men, thinking back to the last dispute, suggested
arbitration: the owners, whose memories were no shorter,
refused. Crawshay of the Cyfarthfa Mine put the view of many in
his blunt reply that he was his own arbitrator. The men, in turn,
refused to accept the reduction and 60,000 were locked out. The
dispute dragged on for three months, while the strike funds were
steadily depleted, until the men accepted a compromise. The
owners, sensing that they had the Union on the run, hardly waited
for the men to get back to work before announcing a further wage
reduction. The locked-out men were demoralized, hungry,
lacking in resources. They went back on the owners' terms. The
owners were now ready to turn defeat into a rout. In December
1874 wages were cut yet again and the men came out. Tom Halliday,
the President of the Amalgamated Association of Miners, came
down from Lancashire to help organize the strikers: funds were
sent from the Union and contributions came in from other districts,
including more than £1,000 from Durham. The owners, following
the maxim of attack being the best form of defence, rather than
attempting to reach a compromise announced that instead of a 10
per cent reduction the cut was to be 15 per cent. Many of the men
panicked. The unity of the strikers was smashed, and eventually
they all had to return, accepting a humiliating $2\frac{1}{2}$ per cent reduc-

tion. The owners' objective was reached — the power of the Amalgamated Association of Miners in South Wales was broken.

The South Wales disputes and similar actions in Staffordshire and Lancashire were major factors in the breaking of the Amalgamated Association of Miners. But it had fought well and had shown that, given unity and resources, the power of the owners could be withstood. A new and stronger body was to develop in its place.

SAVED FROM STANLEY DISASTER

Accident and Disaster

Top left: There was great hope of improvement when Sir Humphry Davy invented his safety-lamp, which he is shown demonstrating, and it gave some protection. Left: Eventually, every mine had a store similar to this at Pontypridd. Above: Every miner collected and checked his lamp before descending.

Previous page: One hundred and sixty-eight died at Stanley in 1909, these few were saved.

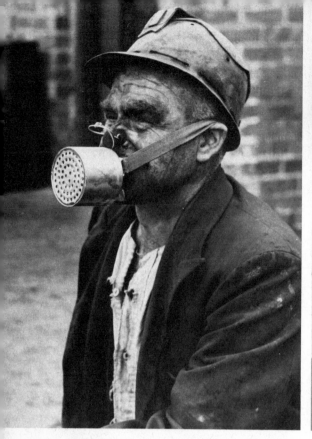

A great danger after an explosion was poison gas. This astonishingly crude 'self rescuer' dates from 1953.

The canary was about to be taken down the William Pit at Whitehaven following an explosion in 1947.

FUN.—December 29, 1866.

BRITANNIA AT BARNSLEY.

Britannia (to the Widows and Orphans):—"I CANNOT SIT DOWN BY MY CHRISTMAS FIRE UNTIL I HAVE DONE SOMETHING FOR YOU!"

In spite of the Davy lamp explosions not only continued but became worse. The Victorians made public wail but the horror continued: Britannia in 1866 seemed content with charity for the victims.
The twentieth century sa more tragedy. This illustrated poem was sold to raise money for the families of the Stanley miners in 1909.

West Stanley Colliery Disaster.

Tuesday, February 16th, 1909.   (Total Death Roll 168).

The Wail of Woe.   *(Copyright)*.

Hark to that agonizing wail
From broken hearts whose spirits fail,
They mourn and weep in deep despair
And cries of anguish rend the air.

In Ramah such a voice was heard
A mother's soul was strangely stirred,
Unutterably sad her lot,
Whom she had borne and loved, were not.

To-day across our native plains
We hear these mournful plaintive strains,
Like to the ocean's direful dirge
When troubled waves around us surge.

The husband, father, brother, son,
Resumed his toil; their course is run :
Within the piercèd hand of love
We leave them, till we meet above.

And as our lamentations rise,
O Lord send succour from the skies ;
Bind up the wounds, assuage the smart,
And stanch the tears that scalding start.

And help us through our fleeting days,
In heart and life, to show Thy praise ;
Forgive our sins, and may we stand
Pardoned and pure, at Thy right hand.

Wesleyan Methodist Manse, Kilsyth, N.B.
18th February, 1909.

R. ERNEST LITTLE.

PRICE : ONE PENNY (Total Proceeds in aid of Stanley Disaster Fund).

Printed gratis by R. Jackson & Co., *Guardian* Office, Consett.   Wholesale at usual trade terms of Messrs. C. C. Ross Ltd.
Side, Newcastle ; Messrs. W. H. Smith and Sons, Forth Place, Newcastle, or of the Printers.

Top: The crowds at Whitehaven gather to watch and wait. Above: At the end of it all, the lists of the dead are posted: 104 were killed, only 3 survived. Right: Widows and children remain.

Above: The dead are buried.

Right: The scenes of disaster do not change. The women wait at Easington in 1951.

Far right and below: Women press forward to see who has survived at Knockshinock in 1950.

Left: Injured men are helped from the pit at Agecroft, 1958, after being trapped for seven hours. Right: The greatest tragedy of all comes when hopes are abandoned. At Michael Colliery, Scotland, three men were still trapped when fire and smoke made all further attempts at rescue impossible.

Mine safety has come a long way since these men were at work at Ryehope.

New helmet testing is dramatic but convincing.

Left: Dr Bronowski was the Director of the Central Research Establishment and is seen here, in 1951, investigating the causes of a fire at Cresswell Pit. Right: Propaganda stressed the importance of safety.

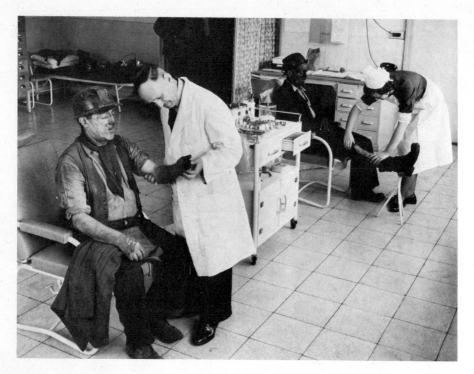

Above: Many mines have their own medical centres. The blackened men seemed
oddly out of place in the antiseptic cleanliness of Easington's Centre.
Below: Tragedy can still touch all sections of the mining community.
In October 1966 an obscene flood of slime came down from the mountain of
colliery spoil to engulf the children of Aberfan.

Chapter Seven

The Search for Safety

Following the Felling disaster, the Sunderland Committee had been formed, had supervised the arrangements for obtaining a satisfactory safety-lamp and, when that had been achieved, had disbanded. As far as the public was concerned, the question of mine safety had been resolved. Few outside the mining districts knew differently, few knew that rather than decreasing the number of mine accidents was steadily increasing. In Galloway's *Annals of Coal Mining and the Coal Trade*, there are details of explosions in the various regions for the period 1836 to 1850. The list, with brief details, extends over ninety-four pages.

Page after page repeats the same story of explosion, death, and injury. Sometimes the story is of a great explosion, sometimes only property was damaged and none of the men and boys were injured. Nevertheless the story of human destruction is terrible. Galloway records more than 600 separate explosions, and makes no pretence of recording all, and from those he reports more than 1,700 deaths. Again, the list is incomplete, as entry after entry records 'much injured' or 'severely burned', so that given the state of medical care the eventual death-roll must have been considerably higher. The *Merthyr Guardian* voiced the plea of many: 'If science has discovered a remedy, in the name of poor widows and fatherless children, we ask, why not make use of it?'

Science had come along with part of the answer in the Davy lamp. The safety precautions were known, what was lacking was the will to make men follow them. The gas that exploded was more often than not there because the mine had bad ventilation, or had not been ventilated while not in use. The actual explosion came in the great majority of cases from the use of naked lamps. How could it happen? The short answer is that it was no one's responsibility to see that it did not happen. A tragic example could be seen at Ardsley Main Colliery in March 1847. Seventy-three died in the accident, caused by using a naked flame in a waste part of the mine. At the inquest, the jury very reasonably brought in this verdict: 'Accidental death, and the jury are of opinion that efficient regulations are not enforced in this district, to prevent the use of naked lights in those parts of coal mines where inflammable gas is known to exist; and are further of the opinion, that the recurrence of accidents involving so large a loss of human life, demands the immediate attention of Her Majesty's Government, and would justify Parliament in framing such a code of regulations as would give greater security to persons employed in mining operations.' The jury asked for their views to be made known to the Secretary of State. For all the effect it had at that time, they might as well have asked for their views to be made known to the Man in the Moon. So little effect did their words have that less than two years were to pass before another major tragedy struck the Yorkshire town. On the morning of 24 January 1849, a great column of smoke and coal-dust rose from the shaft at Darley Main, Barnsley. Seventy-five were killed in this second disaster.

Reading page after page of accounts of explosions caused by naked lights, it seems natural to ask: 'What sort of idiots continued to work like this, when the results were so well known?' The question might seem merely rhetorical, but in fact the answer was more complex than it might appear. In part it could be answered by asking another question – 'What sort of employers sent men to work in mines full of dangerous gas?' For the men who went into the gas-filled mines were paid by results which took no account of conditions – the temptation to substitute the comparatively bright flame of the candle for the dull glow of the safety-lamp was strong for men struggling to earn a semblance of a livelihood. In any case there is a very common human response to accidents – they always happen to someone else. Why else should so many car-drivers, in spite of publicity, continue to drive without safety-belts? Why else should so many, in spite of the clear cancer dangers, continue to smoke? The nineteenth-century miner was hardly more idiotic than the twentieth-century citizen, and he had a more reasonable excuse. Even today we have not solved all problems of mine accidents. Incomplete though the records may be, it is very clear that many of the accidents were caused by the careless-ness of children in the mines. It is a terrifying thought that the safety and lives of dozens, even hundreds, of men and boys could depend on the carefulness of an unsupervised child – a child who today would still be in primary school.

In the circumstances, the suggestion that Parliament might pass legislation to insist on safety measures being taken seems neither extreme nor unreasonable. Parliament had already considered problems of mine safety through a Select Committee in 1835, but the suggestion that the Government should interfere in any way with the owners' rights to do whatever they pleased with their own mines was greeted with such howls of outrage that that particular suggestion was very speedily dropped. However, with the passing of Lord Ashley's Bill in 1842, an Inspector was appointed to see that the law was obeyed. The fact that he was only one man required to investigate hundreds of mines and that his powers to insist on seeing underground workings were so loosely defined that the Inspector never made use of them, was perhaps less important in the long term than the simple fact of his existence. A Government official was there and, in theory at any rate, had the power to interfere in the autocracy of the mine-owners. A new principle had come to mining.

The idea of a mines inspectorate was widely canvassed in the 1840s, not least by the Association of Miners, but attempts to turn idea into law failed. Disasters such as Darley Main brought the matter into prominence, but the arguments and wrangles went on until interest faded and the dead were safely buried. But on 5 June 1849 another major explosion, this time at Hebburn Colliery, Newcastle, again stirred Parliament and this time the stirrings led to more positive action. The miners themselves were determined not to let the Honourable Members ignore them any longer. They used occasions such as the opening of the London Coal Exchange to placard the City to make their views known, and they published a whole series of monthly pamphlets 'on the necessity of legislative interference'. On 10 August 1850 the Act for the Inspection of Coal Mines in Great Britain received the Royal Assent. It provided for the appointment of inspectors and, for the first time, called for the official registration of all mine accidents. It was something less than the miners had wished for. Only four inspectors were appointed to cover the whole of Britain, and, although they were empowered by the legislature to inspect mines and advise mine-owners on safety measures, there was nothing in the legislation to ensure that the owners listened. Another of the miners' not unreasonable suggestions – that those responsible for inspecting and supervising mines should have some training and qualification for the job – was ignored. But the miners continued to agitate and the following year saw the establishment of the Royal School of Mines. All in all it was a faint-hearted gesture towards saving the lives of thousands and preserving many thousands more from serious injury. But it was a start.

What difference did the 1850 Act make to the safety of men in the mines? Sadly, very little. Papers such as the *British Miner* regularly reported accidents and what one notices is not so much the great disasters that made national news, but the continuous stream of small accidents: small accidents, but big enough to cause death and injury. There are stories of rock falls, floodings, explosions, accidents in the shaft, runaway tubs on the underground railway. There are also the bitter complaints about the ineffectiveness of the new laws. Report after report makes the same point – the majority of accidents could have been prevented.

Some of the worst mining disasters were those which need not, and should not, have happened. Cymmer Colliery: the Inspector told the owners of the need for better ventilation and safety-lamps, but no action was taken – 115 killed. Lundhill Colliery, again no safety-lamps were used — 189 killed. Worst of all was Hartley Colliery. There the beam of the pumping engine broke, half of the giant metal structure falling down the only shaft, knocking away the brattice-work, sealing the shaft, and destroying all ventilation and all means of escape. In the tomb of Hartley, 204 miners perished. At last Parliament was again stirred to action and an Act was passed which compelled the owners to provide at least two shafts for every pit. In spite of these legislative forays, the story of mine accidents seems too often to be one that can most charitably be described as gross negligence.

The *British Miner* carried a full account in December 1862 of the events leading up to yet another explosion that hit unhappy Barnsley. Work at the Edmunds' Main Colliery had been pushed along hard: the men were getting bonuses and were winning 50 yards of coal a fortnight. The danger signs were soon written plainly in the pit. At each blasting there were regular fires and extra men were brought down to control them. The technique was hopelessly inadequate, the men going to the fire and putting it out by 'knocking it about with their jackets'. On the Saturday before the accident, the fire burned a whole hour before the men could beat it out. The blasting went on, but on the Monday the fire was not to be quenched. For an hour and a half the men fought the flames until it was obvious that the struggle was hopeless. Those who could escaped: fifty-three died. At the inquest it was agreed that the method of working the pit was 'incautious and unsafe' but the coroner refused to allocate any blame. In an editorial, the *British Miner* reacted angrily to the verdict, demanding that those guilty of negligence should pay the price. The correspondence columns put the same point even more vigorously: 'The preventive powers of the Act are not and never have been enforced; we want inspection prior to accidents. Sham inquests before mining engineers and viewers, and occasional paltry prosecutions of the small fry in the management afterwards, are ridiculous and ineffective for the prevention of accidents . . . the present inspection system is a sham, a farce, and a fallacy; and every intelligent miner knows it.'

It is easy to ask why the inspectorate did not make greater efforts to ensure proper working of mines, but at an inquest following an explosion at the Cwmpenna Colliery, the Inspector for South Wales explained that, working full time, it took him three and a half years to visit every colliery in his district. The plea for punitive measures against owners and overseers had little enough chance of success. The Barnsley verdict was typical, and one correspondent quoted a case where eleven of an inquest jury found a colliery overseer guilty of negligence and manslaughter. The twelfth, a mining engineer like the accused, disagreed. The coroner accepted the version of the one and set aside the views of the eleven. Workmen accused of negligence found a different attitude; magistrates suddenly became zealous guardians of mine safety. A Wigan miner, for example, found with a pipe in his pocket, was sent to gaol. Nineteenth-century literature often describes the miners as lawless. What else should they be when the law was seen as little better than an instrument of prejudice and privilege?

It was not as if the law attempted to show even a semblance of impartiality. When the 1850 Act was renewed in 1855, provisions for new safety regulations were incorporated and a scale of punishments was laid down. Owners and supervisors could be punished by fines, workmen by imprisonment. The legislators could argue, persuasively enough, that to impose fines on workmen was equivalent to sending them to prison, since they would never have enough cash to pay the fines. However it might have seemed to the Members of Parliament, to the ordinary workmen it seemed just one more example of injustice and did little for the cause of safety. Matters were made worse by some owners who, told they could introduce the legally enforceable safety regulations, came up with such rules as compulsory church attendance. It was not until 1872 that real progress was made and some equality of treatment introduced when an Act was passed which made it compulsory for all mine managers to pass a Government examination of competence. The same Act strengthened safety regulations and went a long way to introducing much-needed reforms, including compulsory schooling for mine boys.

If the history of miners and mining is in large measure a history of a war fought against a deadly environment, then it is at least a war fought with great heroism. The early accounts of disasters and accidents rarely mention the actions and feelings of the men and women of the mining communities. One notable exception is a book *Buried Alive!* written in 1877 by an eyewitness, Charles Williams, who describes in great detail the accident and the rescue operation at Tynewydd Pit in the Rhondda on 11 April of that year.

The men were working very close to the flooded number three seam of the Cymmer Pit when suddenly the barrier broke and the waters rushed in to Tynewydd. Most of the men scrambled their way to safety as the flood swept in, but fourteen remained below ground. The four nearest the break were killed instantly, but two other groups of five struggled to safety.

As soon as it was clear that there were men left below ground, the rescue attempt began. The first group of five were soon located in their pocket of air between the coal-face and the water, and the men began at once to hack at the barrier of coal. Sadly, they had not allowed for the great force of the pent-up air and as soon as the breakthrough was made, the rush of the air hurled one of the trapped men against the face and he died at the moment of escape. The other four were brought safely out of the mine.

The hunt for the remaining five began on the Thursday, and on the following day knocking was heard from Thomas Morgan's stall. Between the rescuers and the trapped men there was a 38-yard barrier of coal, which could only be approached down roadways turned into a vast underground sea. The alternative was to try and reach them through the main floodwater, and divers came who volunteered to attempt to travel the 257 yards of passages flooded from floor to ceiling. They tried and failed. It was clear that if there was to be a rescue, then a way would have to be forced through the coal barrier. Pumping at once began to lower the water-level so that work could begin. Only four miners at a time could get into the face, and they worked three- to four-hour shifts.

'They rained down blow after blow unremittingly; no halt, no looking back, no word; fiercely, almost savagely, the men worked, and when the shift of three hours had passed, only fell back exhausted for fresh men to advance again, and show that the same grand stimulus inspired them, prompting to the same desperate hardihood and determination.' By the Wednesday they could clearly hear the knocking from the other side of the barrier, but just as it seemed that they would soon be through, gas began seeping into the workings. Twice the miners were driven from the face and had to wait while the engineers adjusted the ventilation to sweep away the gas before they could return. Again the breakthrough was almost a disaster. Air began to rush through the hole and the water began rising rapidly, threatening to engulf the five survivors. Hastily the hole was replugged while the engineers worked out how to make the breakthrough in such a way that the trapped men could pass through the gap before the waters rose too high.

All through the rescue operation, the men kept continuously at the task. 'Most wonderful were the endurance and action of the colliers. It was a noticeable feature that, beating against the black face of coal, which any moment might open out and destroy them, they never turned their heads. With blood streaming, in the earlier part of the week, from their hands, they yet rained blow after blow and, said a looker on, never turned or paused.' They worked under the double threat of inundation or explosion, but no one hesitated. And it was not only the colliers who worked – agents, engineers, owners, all came down to help with pumps and ventilating doors. On the Friday, the attempt was made. The coal-face was broken in, gas and air rushed out like a hurricane, and, before the waters could fill their refuge, the five prisoners were pulled to safety.

The five who came out after more than a week's entombment were at last able to tell their own story. They had been without food for the whole of the time and only survived by drinking the floodwater that lapped round them. Two of the men became half-crazed from their ordeal and one of them, John Thomas, 'kept staring to where the water was and struggling to get away, calling out, "Let me go; I see a hole that I can get away through."' Only the firmness of George Jenkins and Moses Powell, the two men who kept tight control throughout the time, prevented him from walking away, down into the black water. The fifth was a young boy, David Hughes, who later told Williams of how Jenkins and Powell cared for him. 'The men there saved my life. They nursed me all the time. I was kept warm by sleeping in their laps.' David Hughes had only one plea to make at the end of his story – that he should never again have to go down the mine.

The Tynewydd accident was not exceptionally bad, nor the rescue exceptionally heroic: it is mainly notable for having been so carefully recorded. But death and injury were familiar enough in every mining village, and the endurance, the carelessness of danger shown by the rescuers, were repeated a hundredfold with no one on hand to record them. Although Williams hardly mentions it, this common experience of sharing hardship, of facing death, drew the mining community together by uniquely strong bonds. When the news of a pit accident reached the village, everyone felt it as a personal disaster. Each wife knew that her husband or her sons stood in the same danger. So too, the rescuers were working to save friends and relations. These strong bonds were reinforced by the nature of the mining village and its community. They were isolated, with the mine often the only source of employment. Miners, looked upon almost as a race apart, ignored by the rest of the world, were content to draw inwards, to make their own lives. Probably only the fishing villages, which shared the same sense of isolation and shared danger and loss, could show a comparable unity of outlook and feeling. There were many differences between the miner of South Wales and his counterpart in Scotland, between a village in Nottinghamshire and one in Northumberland, but in much they were the same.

From the nature of mining and the mining community there developed the two strong pillars on which the organization of the miners came to be built – self-sufficiency and unity of purpose. The miners had lived and grown up in isolation and were prepared, if need be, to fight for their rights in isolation. And, in the long history of accident and disaster, they had learned to support each other. Towards the end of the nineteenth century, a new and powerful structure was set up on those supports.

Struggle

Right: the great events of the Union's history are recorded round the edge of this diploma awarded for fifty years of membership. Below: The Unions came, and the heroes of the movement are celebrated on the banners of the miners' lodges.

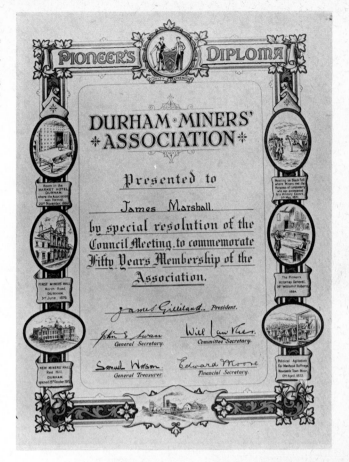

Opposite: For the unemployed, there were the long miserable marches.

Above: The miners have had to face hardship and brutality. This Ryehope family are camped out in the street because they had been evicted by the owners for striking. Left: Among the bleakest times were those in the 1930s when men suffered the horrors of mass unemployment. These South Wales miners tried to run their own small mine.

Marches took their toll in shoe leather.

A mass rally in Hyde Park in 1934.

The Second World War ended unemployment, and afterwards the miners saw the realization of one of their great ambitions. The mines were nationalized. The Labour Prime Minister, Attlee, made a speech, watched by that great miners' MP, Aneurin Bevan.

Left: On 7 January 1947, a new flag was hoisted over the mines of Britain. Above: With the band playing, the banners flying, the men marched in celebration of nationalization. Below: Nationalization did not mean instant peace in the coalfields. These men are watching fellow strikers from Grimethorpe and South Kirby play each other at cricket. The year is 1947.

The post-war years saw a new threat to miners' livelihoods – pit closures. Below: At Waleswood in Yorkshire in 1948, the men stayed down in protest against closure. Left: The families at Waleswood prepared food for the men. They gained a little time. Above: These men of Aberdare were leaving their pit for the last time in January 1959.

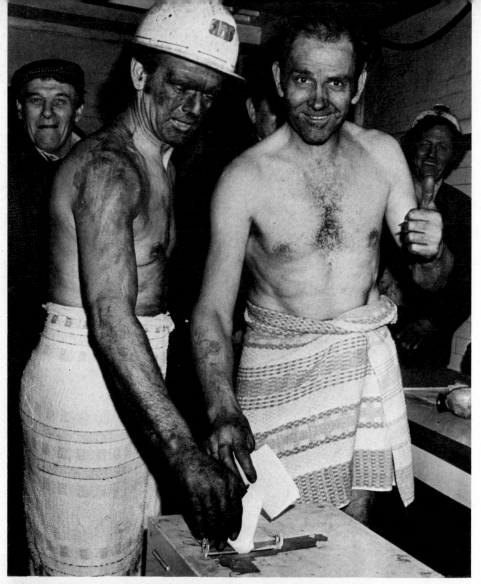

Above: The 1970s saw new demands for coal, and in 1974 the miners showed their power. They voted to strike and the Government fell.

Below: The miners' leaders, Lawrence Daly, Joe Gormley, and Mick McGahey went to see the new Employment Secretary.

Above: What had started as a protest march in Macclesfield turned
into a victory parade. Below: The Miners' Unions have their own
special days of celebration – Gala Days. Here the crowds gather for
the Durham Gala of 1908 (the x is over the head of the local MP).

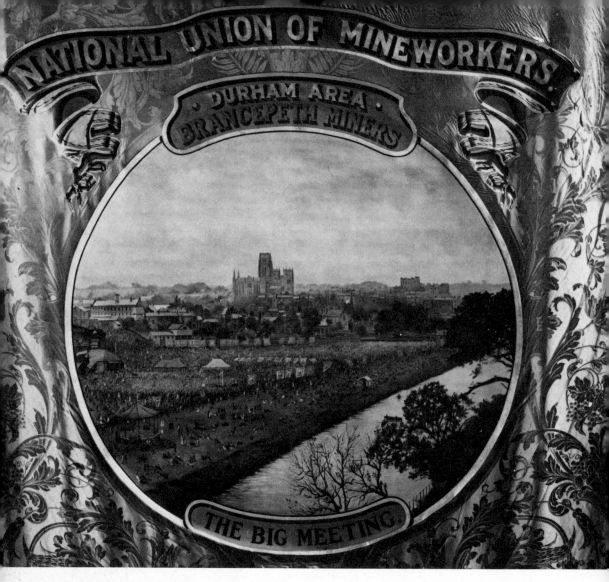

The whole panorama of a Durham Gala
is shown on this fine banner.

Chapter Eight
Union

Following the defeat of the miners' strikes in the early 1870s, the Amalgamated Association of Miners went into a decline and eventually disappeared as an active organization. In the place of the Union and Union leaders, the men's bargaining was left to a new organization and a new type of leader. In coalfield after coalfield the miners entered into sliding-scale agreements, which tied wages to coal prices and left bargaining to the Sliding Scale Committee.

Lloyd James, Trade Unionist, journalist, and politician was one of many who argued against the acceptance of sliding scales that were not buttressed by a minimum wage agreement. 'The present agreements they are going into on fluctuating market prices is a practical placing of their fate in the hands of others. It is throwing the bread of their children into a scramble of competition where everything is decided by the blind and selfish struggle of their employers.' For the representatives of the men on the Committee the position was impossible: they were servants of two masters. All might have been well if the economy had been booming, but instead the economy slumped and wages fell with the price of coal. Old sliding scales were replaced by new, even less favourable. Scales and wages sank steadily lower.

There were strikes against wage reductions, and attempts to forge a unity among the miners. Lancashire men supported strikers in Staffordshire in 1883 by raising a levy to provide them with funds. Mine leaders stressed the importance of unity, as in this handbill, quoted in R. P. Arnot's *The Miners*. The language is melodramatic, but the message clear.

'Shall we not buckle on our armour afresh and fight with greater vigour? The battle at present is being fought in Staffordshire, but if we are beaten there, we shall have to either fight in Lancashire or surrender. The Levy may be considered by some men very heavy, but the reduction will be threefold more. Who amongst our ranks would rather give the employers 2s. than the men 8d?' But the support was too limited, and the battle was lost.

The only body which could claim any widespread organization was the National Union, which drew almost all its support from the north-east of England. The National Union were firm believers in sliding scales, in their ability to co-operate with the owners for their mutual benefit, and in Parliament. In the last case they had some successes and important successes at that. The minimum age at which boys could be employed underground was raised to twelve and, what was to prove of great importance for future generations of Trade Unionists and labour leaders, they managed to establish the rights of miners to appoint checkweighmen who, as their name suggests, were responsible for checking the weight of coal which a miner brought to bank. In the short term this was important for controlling the abuses of the pit-head and ensuring that men received fair pay for the work they performed. In the long term it was important, for it enabled the miners to get their leaders into positions of authority. But the slump hit the sliding scales of the north-east every bit as hard as it hit those of the rest of Britain, and the inability of either the fragmented local Unions or the moderate National Union to fight the steady decline in pay led many to look to a new form of Unionism for the mines.

Towards the end of the 1880s the state of the miners' organizations could reasonably be described as chaotic. Union membership was low, in some areas virtually non-existent. All kinds of new ideas were being discussed and tried. Some looked to the comparatively new doctrines of Socialism. Others tried to analyse the economic forces that were pulling down wages. One apparently obvious answer was that there was simply too much coal: reduce the quantity and the price and thus wages would rise. The next step was to renew agitation for an old mining demand – the eight-hour day. There was a rhyme they used to sing in Yorkshire that put it neatly and succinctly:

Eight hours' work
Eight hours' play
Eight hours' sleep
And eight bob a day.

There was also a growing feeling that some sort of action was needed, and that to succeed such action should be concerted. In one sense, the time seemed inauspicious, as depression and poverty were on public view wherever one looked. Ben Pickard, the Yorkshire mine leader, looked back on those days in 1887 when 'in most of the mining districts, low wages and starvation both in regard to food and to clothing ruled. As I proceeded from one mining village to another and saw the destitution and impoverished condition of the people, with the children going about barefoot and bare-legged up and down the little streets, I came to the conclusion that better things should be the lot of the mining population. The more villages I entered and the more information I obtained, confirmed me in the determination to rouse the people, not merely in Yorkshire, but throughout the country.'

On 10 September 1888, Ben Pickard sent out an invitation for representatives of all miners' organizations that were not tied by sliding-scale agreements to meet together to discuss ways in which they could all act to demand a 10 per cent increase in wages. A fortnight later the meeting took place at the Co-operative Hall at Ardwick with delegates from Yorkshire, Lancashire, Derbyshire, Nottinghamshire, and Leicestershire, North Wales, Stirling, and a few smaller groups in the Midlands. They passed a resolution agreeing to demand a 10 per cent rise backed by a strike threat and then arranged to meet again two days after the deadline of 27 October to see how the owners had responded. The move was well timed. The slump was ending and almost all the owners paid the 10 per cent with little argument – only Derbyshire and Yorkshire owners refused to pay. At once the other areas began to raise a levy to support the Yorkshire and Derbyshire strikers, and within days the raise was granted. The message could not have been plainer. As Pickard's message from the October conference put it: 'Remember, by Unity we got the advance, and by Unity we may preserve it.'

The danger facing the miners was a split between the new, loose federation which had demonstrated its strength in pay negotiations, and the old National Union. But the National Union seemed unconcerned – they saw their role entirely in terms of Parliament prodding and were not too worried about the growth of another body that would pursue wage claims. Their chance of retaining an exclusive control over all matters concerning legislation began to look a little slender when, at a miners' national conference in Birmingham in 1889, the Secretary of the comparatively tiny Ayrshire Union, with a membership of 1,000 out of a work force of 10,000, argued for the discussion of an Eight Hours Bill and other Parliamentary questions. He made it quite plain that such matters were every bit as much the concern of militant Unionists as they were of moderates and he was later to gain fame for his advocacy of a new Parliamentary party that would represent the interests of working people. The Secretary, a comparatively unknown figure at the Birmingham conference, was James Keir Hardie.

The main concern in 1889 was still to push ahead on the wages front, and again, though strike action was needed in some areas and more than £11,000 was paid out in strike funds, they won their 10 per cent. The new organization had earned its spurs. A meeting was called at Newport, Monmouthshire – Newport in the heart of the South Wales coalfield, where the heavy defeats had broken the back of the old Association, in the coalfield where Unionism was weakest and sliding-scale agreements strongest. It was an impudent act of nose-thumbing towards the dictatorial South Wales mineowners, and the mark of growing self-confidence. On 26 November the resolution was passed that gave formal acknowledgment to what had already been accomplished – the Miners' Federation of Great Britain was formed. For half a century the M.F.G.B. was to speak for the miners of Britain.

The Federation at once began to agitate for an eight-hour-day Bill, and the agitation inevitably strengthened the growing rift between the north-east and the districts represented in the M.F.G.B. At the same time the Federation continued successfully to push ahead with wage claims. While prices rose it was not difficult to push up wages, but when prices began to fall again then the Federation had to remove its attention from working hours as an old foe appeared over the horizon – wage reduction. At first the owners were content to snipe at the weaker regions, leaving the Federation collieries untouched, but in 1893 battle was joined. The rifts in the movement deepened, but the M.F.G.B. was left no weaker than it had been at formation and determined not to yield one penny of wages in any pit. The reduction notices were given to the men, the terms were refused, and the great lock-out began. The Federation put on a display of confidence, but the leaders must have been desperately worried that their new organization would crumble under the attack. They put the owners' terms to the men. To the question: 'Will you agree to 25 per cent reduction in wages, or any part thereof?', a mere 221 replied 'yes', while 143,695 replied 'no'. The Federation now knew that, beyond any question, they spoke for the miners. The struggle was to be both bloody and bitter.

The lock-out was six weeks' old when the miners of Featherstone, Yorkshire, heard that poor-quality coal was being loaded by surface workers at Lord Masham's Ackton Hall Colliery. Two hundred men marched to the pit to complain: there was an argument, some trucks were overturned and the men left. The manager at once rushed off to Pontefract to demand police protection. Unfortunately, the police had more important matters in hand and were fully occupied at Doncaster Races. However, Lord St Oswald, who was a Featherstone mine-owner, also appeared on the scene and added his voice to the demands for protection. The manager might have had little success on his own, but Lord St Oswald was also a JP and a man of some importance. The Chief Constable politely suggested that troops might be called in, at which Lord St Oswald immediately donned his magisterial authority and gave the order for the troops to be summoned.

The soldiers duly arrived to find that there was no crowd to disperse, but as they took up positions at the colliery one soon emerged, anxious to discover what was happening. Tension mounted, stones were thrown at the engine-house, and a pile of timber was set on fire. The military presence had caused the riot it was designed to prevent. The Captain in charge of the soldiers showed himself to be too sensible a man to stay in such an absurd situation and, after talking to the rioters, it was agreed that the crowd would disperse and the soldiers leave.

Had the common sense of Captain Barker and the miners prevailed, the name Featherstone would have remained as a footnote to the story of the 1893 lock-out. Sadly, the Captain was met at the railway station by a less sensible man – Mr Hartley, a Pontefract magistrate. The soldiers were sent back to the colliery and again a crowd assembled. This time Mr Hartley was on hand to read the Riot Act, which he proceeded to do. The crowd took little notice and the order was given for the soldiers to fire into the crowd: two were killed and sixteen injured. The crowd remained. At that point another troop of soldiers arrived, and at last the crowd broke up. If the extra soldiers had not come, the situation could well have become even worse. It was, in all conscience, bad enough. The magistrates by their senseless and provocative actions called a crowd into being and when that same crowd had not gone away again they had ordered the Army to fire. It seemed as if the clock of industrial unrest had whirred backwards for half a century.

The lock-out continued and families were brought to the edge of starvation. But now the story follows very different lines from those of the bleakest days of the early part of the century. Public sympathy was with the miners and help began to appear – money, clothes, goods poured in to be distributed by the Federation. Soup-kitchens were set up and run by the miners. Gradually owners, too, began to give way. In the past it had been the steady trickle back to work that had ended strikes – now it was a trickle back but on the men's terms. And every man back at work meant a double gain: he and his family drew no money from the strike funds; he could put money into the funds out of his wages. It was clear that the men would not be easily broken. In the event, the trial of strength was brought to an end by Government intervention. After the failure of attempted conciliation by the Board of Trade, Gladstone himself stepped in and proposed that an arbitrator should be appointed. The job went to no less a person than the Foreign Secretary, Lord Rosebery. Both sides agreed to the arbitration and on 17 November, sixteen weeks after the start of the dispute, the result was announced. The men were to return to work at the old rates. For them it was a complete victory. Thomas Ashton, the M.F.G.B. Secretary recalled the effect on the miners when there was 'singing, dancing, shouting, laughing and crying for joy, and in several districts the church bells were set ringing to celebrate the great event'. Rosebery himself wrote in his diary: 'Dined alone, very tired. But it would have been a good day to die on.'

The Federation still did not represent all British miners, one notable absentee being the great body of men working in the pits of South Wales. They were still firmly bound to the sliding scale, but as their living standards declined and as conditions deteriorated, the South Wales miners' patience finally gave and they sent in a demand for a 10 per cent rise and for the ending of the scale. The owners' response was immediate: they gave the men notice of a lock-out to begin in April 1898. The pattern was similar in some ways to the 1893 strike: the military were brought in as a force of occupation to keep a peace which had neither been broken nor threatened, and the miners settled down for the customary war of attrition with the owners. But the Welsh lacked the organizational unity of the strikers of 1893 and, more important, they lacked the backing of other districts. In the end they were defeated, but they had learned a lesson. The following year Wales was in the M.F.G.B. Edward Cowey of Yorkshire, who seconded the motion of acceptance of the Welsh into the Federation, expressed the views of all the executive, especially perhaps the President, Ben Pickard, who had fought long and hard for unity: 'We have made many attempts and many tries to get our Welsh brethren to join. I must admit that we had almost given up hope. But now the time has arrived; and I am exceedingly pleased, as one of the founders of this Federation, that this time has arrived and our friends have now joined us. It will help to make us one of the most powerful federations in this country that has ever been seen.'

The successes of the Federation were its greatest strength in recruiting district and local Unions, and in 1908 the north-east finally abandoned the old National Union. First Northumberland and then Durham joined the Federation; the days of the two Unions were finally ended. The miners of Great Britain spoke with one voice, and that voice was raised that same year in a resounding cheer that was heard in every colliery in the land. After years of opposition, followed by years of political shilly-shallying, the miners won their years-long battle. The Eight Hours Bill became law. First the National Union had fought, then the Federation had added its weight, all the time facing a continuous and voluble opposition from the owners. It was not quite the Bill that the miners demanded, which would have limited the hours to eight from bank to bank, that is from the time of starting down the pit to the time of returning to the surface. Instead, winding time was excluded from the eight hours, so that men in the deepest pits with the longest roadways could still work over the time for no extra pay. But that was a small criticism to set against the greatness of the prize, won over such a length of time and after such a struggle.

The years leading up to the First World War saw one of the major disputes in the mining industry, where the Federation demonstrated its strength and cohesion in a national strike that closed almost every pit in Britain. The issue was the minimum wage. It was an issue of great importance to the miners, who were often on piece rates. Their earnings were not dependent on their own efforts so much as on the physical geography of the coalfield in which they worked. A man could find himself in a stall, his section of the coalface, which was high and wide, with a face of good coal. The earnings were rich and the end of the week a small bonanza. That was one side of the picture. A second man might be put to work in a seam scarcely more than 2 feet high, a seam where the coal was crushed into unprofitably small pieces. Often such places required extra timbering to shore up the roof against possible collapse. This man, in his week's work, would have to labour under far more difficult conditions than the first, yet his rewards would be smaller, so small even that they might not be sufficient to keep him and his family from wretched poverty and near-starvation. The problem was exacerbated by the system of allocating the work: it was too easy for a supervisor to pay off old scores by consistently sending a man to what were known as 'abnormal places'. So to the miners this was no academic bargaining-point. There was a deep resentment against a system that could take two men, set them to work, and reward or penalize them for virtues or faults which were none of their own making. The owners resisted the proposal.

The strike began at the end of February 1912. The Government were horrified at the thought that the nation might suddenly find itself coalless. Recent events have shown the continued importance of coal, but in 1912 that importance could be doubled, even trebled. Industry was still dependent on the steam-engine, fired by coal; bulk transport meant rail transport and the steam locomotive, fired by coal; homes were lit by coal-gas, warmed by coal-fires. There was hardly an aspect of British life in which coal did not play a vital role. It is hardly surprising that the Government were not prepared to leave the issue to be settled by resolute miners and intractable coal-owners. The Government hastily brought out their own proposals for a minimum wages Bill that evoked no enthusiasm in either camp. There was to be no national minimum wage, which was what the miners wanted, but minimum rates were to be set by Joint Boards of employers and miners under an impartial chairman, negotiating at district level. The details mattered less to the employers than the basic idea: all talk of a minimum wage was anathema to them. Parliament, however, was in no mood to be talked out of its course by either side, and the Bill duly became law.

The Federation was faced with a dilemma. To accept the Act as a solution was to see wage bargaining sent back to the district and an untried and unproved Joint Board. On the other hand, to continue the strike would be to fight against the combined resources of owners and Government and risk losing the very real gain – the acceptance of the justice of a minimum wage. To make matters worse, the Federation's membership was split on the issue. In the event, they decided to try the new Act to see if it could be made to work. For the miners, the result was mixed: the chance to impose national negotiations was lost, and the old-style of piecemeal negotiations was reinforced; but to set against that, the Boards were successful in ensuring a minimum wage for face workers. In the long term, it could be argued that the fragmentation of Union activity proved a major handicap, but to save thousands of men and their families from poverty was no small achievement. For those directly affected it was a victory of sorts. Perhaps such a hastily cobbled-up piece of legislation could never have been expected to bring in any very great satisfaction, though the legislators were happy enough to see a national crisis averted.

The move towards unity was taken a stage further in 1913, when the miners began discussions with other Unions over ways in which they could work together and help each other. From these talks a new alliance was formed between the miners, the National Union of Railwaymen, and the Transport Workers' Federation – the Triple Alliance. The miners were later to find that the new unity of workers had little of the cohesion that came from shared work, shared problems, and shared experience. But it was not yet to be put to the test. In 1914, the Archduke Ferdinand, a ruler of whom few Britons had heard, was assassinated in Sarajevo, a place whose name few Britons could pronounce. The industrial war gave way to the carnage of the Great War.

Opposite: In the nineteenth century, quoits was much in favour.

Time off

The northern miner had his own – and sometimes profitable – sport of Rugby League.

Other hobbies, such as vegetable-growing have always been popular.

Few activities have been more
consistently followed than the
making of music – the Deaf
Hill Temperance Band off to
the Durham Gala in 1924.

The Cresswell Colliery Band
giving an underground concert
in 1970.

Chapter Nine
Below Ground and Above

When the Great War broke out, British mining had reached its peak. From 147,000,000 tons a year in 1880, the industry had expanded so that in 1913 production had almost doubled to 287,000,000 tons. A work force of less than 500,000 in 1880 had grown to 1,250,000 in 1913. A success story? Not if one looks a little closer at the figures, when it becomes apparent that production per man had actually fallen. In the country as a whole the period up to 1913 was one of enormous technological advances – perhaps technological leaps would be a more accurate description. By that year, giant steamships were powering their way across the Atlantic where sail had once ruled; in country lanes, startled horses shied as the new horseless carriages puttered along, driven by the internal-combustion engine; even the skies witnessed a new and miraculous vision as the first, fragile aeroplanes were seen. But under this world of inventiveness and change, the miner continued to work in ways that had scarcely changed for a century.

In the eighteenth century the introduction of the steam-engine revolutionized mining methods, but there were no comparable dramatic changes in the next hundred years. The obvious change one would expect to see, given the general line of development of nineteenth-century industry and engineering, would be the replacement of the man with the pickaxe by a machine. Certainly the mechanical cutter has a long enough history. As early as 1768 a mechanical pick had been tried; the principle was to reproduce the swinging action of a pick-head by means of a system of gears and levers, powered by two men turning a crank. The trouble was the source of power – it was soon obvious that two men and two picks were more efficient than the same two men and a mechanical pick.

Finding a suitable power source for use down a mine was one of the main factors hindering the development of cutters. A circular-saw was tried out in the 1840s and suffered from the same problem, and from not being constructed of a sufficiently high-grade steel. The power problem looked a little nearer solution when compressed air was introduced at Govern Colliery, Glasgow, in 1849, and real progress towards mechanization was made with the introduction of such machines as the Gartsherrie. It was pneumatically powered and had a cutting head on a circular chain mounted on a jib. It undercut the coal-face to a depth of some $4\frac{1}{2}$ feet and could work a 200-yard face in 6 hours, and was manufactured by William Baird and Company of Coatbridge, Scotland in 1864. Despite the technical success of that machine and others like it, some fifty years later as the nineteenth century gave way to the twentieth, machine-cutting still only accounted for 3 per cent of coal production.

The reasons for the slow acceptance of machine-cutting were many and varied. There were technical problems, as compressed air is not a greatly efficient power source and there seem to have been many breakdowns. But the main problem was not technical but organizational. The British coal industry had grown up as literally thousands of independent units, often quite small. These small concerns had no very great capital available for improvements, and, with a steadily growing market for coal, both at home and abroad, and little competition, there was no incentive to indulge in expensive experiments.

So, in the majority of the mines of Britain at the beginning of the First World War, the miner could still be found hewing coal with a pick. In north-east England they still worked the old pillar and stall method, with each man in his own stall, while elsewhere the long-wall method, in which a team advanced along the seam, filling in the space behind them as they went, was usual. Whatever the method of organization used, the work was unchanged. Naked or near-naked, men crouched or lay working at the hard black material with their picks, levering away slabs with their crowbars. Then the putters worked behind the hewers, in the same dark constricted spaces, shovelling the lumps of coal into the waiting tubs. Those of us who complain of aches and pains after a Sunday afternoon's digging in the garden can hardly imagine the effort involved in shovelling coal, hour after hour, in a space where it was often not possible to kneel, let alone stand. True, custom made the work easier to the miner than it would have been to any outsider, but easier is not easy. The line of knobs and scars down the miner's spine told their own story of how working in the low-roofed stalls and seams rubbed the skin from a man's back, bruised and scarred him. At the coal-face, a miner from the eighteenth century would have found little that was remarkable had he returned at the beginning of the twentieth.

The main changes underground were to be seen in the moving of the coal: the wheeled tub had entirely taken over from the old sledges, and tubs could be moved in trains pulled by ponies or by ropes and cables powered by underground engines. The cages hurtled at astonishing speeds in the shafts, reaching a maximum of nearly 50 miles per hour before braking for the bottom. There were no longer women and young children to be employed hauling the corves along the long roadways – the ponies who spent their lives down the mine were now the beasts of burden. Today, we react against the idea of employing animals in such conditions, but until very recently it was a choice between horses and human beings. Yet the ponies had a special place in the affection of the miners, and any old miner – and not so old – has his stories about them. The ponies might be beasts of burden, but they were certainly not mindless ones. One particular pony had a set number of tubs that it would pull. The weight made no difference: full or empty, it would take its due complement of trucks and not one more. And, as with so many aspects of the miner's life, the pony was incorporated into his superstitions. Many miners used the ponies as a kind of forecast for the events of the day: if the pony were fit and in good spirits then the day would go well; but if the pony were ill or restless, then there was trouble ahead for the men who worked with that particular animal. This was taken so seriously that men would actually refuse to work if the pony was ill, convinced that if they did so they would be caught in a rock fall or injured in any one of the many ways in which a man could be hurt down the pit.

The ponies were only one strand in the web of superstition that hemmed in the life of the miner. Some men, for example, would always follow an exact routine when going to work, at least half convinced that any deviation would bring catastrophe. Superstitions may be basically illogical but they are a common response where dangers are constantly threatening, a way of helping to ensure that when disaster struck, it struck somewhere else. And disaster was still all too likely to strike in the mines of Britain in the first decade of the twentieth century.

Mining technology had advanced, and there was a much greater understanding of the dangers of methane gas; but another danger was not understood at all, the danger from coal-dust explosion. There were major explosions at West Stanley in Durham in February 1909 when 168 were killed and in the following year at Whitehaven, Cumberland, killing 136. But worst of all was the explosion at the Senghenydd Colliery in the Aber Valley in October 1913. On that terrible day 439 miners met their death, but it was not until 1920 that regulations came into force to limit the amount of coal-dust in the atmosphere by mixing it with stone-dust or even water. Perhaps a death-rate of 439 in a day seemed less urgent in the intervening years when hundreds of thousands were dying in the mud of Belgium and France.

The miner continued his dirty and dangerous work, but no longer in the total anonymity that there had been in the early nineteenth century. The growth of the miners' organizations, persistent and vocal advocates of their cause, began the process of showing the life of the miner to the rest of the population. Then the miners found their voice in Parliament, first as members of the older parties, then as leaders of the new Labour Party. The presence at Westminster of men such as Keir Hardie ensured that the voice was both loud and persuasive. The growth of education helped miners to speak for themselves, and many men who later became national figures testified to the avidity with which so many miners grasped their opportunity for learning. One aspect of this growing literacy was the tendency of miners and men of the mining community to speak for themselves, to describe their own way of life, their own surroundings and customs.

The most striking feature of early-twentieth-century mining communities is the comparatively slow rate of change. Pit-head baths, for example, were a rarity and little used even where they existed. Partly this was because collieries, such as Wharncliffe in Yorkshire, charged the miners for the use of the baths. The men, reasonably enough, prepared to carry on trudging home in their pit dirt for a free bathe. When the miner did get home, he returned to conditions that showed very little improvement, with over-crowding still common.

One also notices that mining communities still retained their strong individuality, a strong sense of tradition. Accounts of the early-nineteenth-century villages in the north-east tell of the popularity of certain activities – flower- and vegetable-showing, with keen competition for prizes at the local shows, pigeon-racing, music. Not much of that had changed in a century. The brass band was still as popular as ever and, as anyone who has visited a Durham Gala can testify, it still is, though the Northumbrian pipes, which were popular about 1900, have rather disappeared from the musical scene. In 1900, too, old games and traditions were still kept up: quoits and marbles were played; sword-dancing, using five double-handed swords, was popular. Though customs varied between the districts, music has always been a common love of the mining communities, whether pipes, bands, or the male voice choirs of the Welsh valleys. The closed community and the sense of tradition have always tended to go together. All these things had been seen by observers and recorded many times, but what characterizes twentieth-century writing was the emergence of accounts of the private life of the miner, the miner at home, the miner as an individual personality.

In the nineteenth century there were novelists who took an interest in the lives of the working classes, notably Mrs Gaskell. But few paid much attention to the miners. George Eliot's approach in her novel *Felix Holt the Radical* is reasonably typical. She introduces the miners into the story as an ignorant mob, preyed on by every kind of agitator, frequently drunk and often riotous. Although they play an important role, they never emerge as characters nor do we ever learn anything about either their work or their lives away from work. In the early twentieth century there was a great contrast when the son of a miner came to write about the community in which he grew up. D. H. Lawrence was born in 1885 in the village of Eastwood on the Nottingham coalfield. In novels, stories, and plays he wrote of the lives of miners, of pit villages and the relationships between the members of the community. Eastwood appears thinly disguised as Bestwood in the autobiographical novel *Sons and Lovers*. It is soon clear that his view of the miner is strongly coloured by his reactions against his own father, nevertheless Lawrence saw and described scenes of the Nottingham coalfield at the turn of the century with a vividness that was quite new. He caught the atmosphere of the place, presenting it so vividly that it has an almost tangible reality. Take the following brief description from *Lady Chatterley's Lover*:

'From the rather dismal rooms at Wragby she heard the rattle-rattle of the screens at the pit, the puff of the winding-engine, the clink-clink of shunting trucks, and the hoarse little whistle of the colliery locomotives. Tevershall pit-bank was burning, had been burning for years, and it would cost thousands to put it out. So it had to burn. And when the wind was that way, which was often, the house was full of the stench of this sulphurous combustion of the earth's excrement. But even on windless days the air always smelt of something under-earth: sulphur, iron, coal, or acid. And even on the Christmas roses the smuts settled persistently, incredible, like black manna from the skies of doom.'

A novelist such as Lawrence may be less 'reliable' than a historian, but he can create this real awareness of the actuality of life in the villages. We also learn something of the lives of the miners' wives, whether waiting anxiously to see if the men are coming back early on short-time working, with an inevitable pulling in of belts or waiting for them to come home late because of an accident. The ritual of the miner's household first became known to a public outside the villages through the work of writers such as Lawrence and, later, George Orwell. Most Midlands miners still lived in the narrow rows and terraces of two-up-two-down houses. Downstairs, the front room, the parlour, was virtually unused – a showplace no part of living in the house. The kitchen was the centre of all activity. Routine was necessarily tied to the working hours of the mine and, for men working the early shift, the ritual properly begins on the previous night. Then the wife prepared his food – his snap – and his pit-flask for the following day and banked up the fire which, like an Olympian flame, was never allowed to go out inside its shining black grate. Next morning when the men left for work, the village was given over to the community of women. The kitchen at the back of the house opened out on to the yard and the privy, with an ashy alleyway beyond. Across the wall, the women discussed their affairs, while the young children played. In the evening, the men returned home and in the days when pit-head baths were still an undreamed-of luxury, they came back to the tin tub on the hearth to wash themselves and to be washed by their wives. Routine hardly changed except on pay-days, when many men headed for the pub, while the women headed for the market. Lawrence described how, as a young boy suffering from paroxysms of nervousness, he had to wait at the mine agent's office for the pay-packet. He then had to take it to his father who, as a butty, would distribute it among the three or four men in his small gang.

The picture that emerges of the Midlands mining community is of an aggressively masculine world. It is also a picture of a community living very much turned in on itself: between the miners and the rest of the world there was what Lawrence called the 'gulf impassable'. There was also the geographical isolation that could mean, for example, that an injured miner might have to endure a journey of many miles over rutted roads or cobbled streets before reaching hospital or doctor. But there was another side to the mining village. The houses might be dominated by the smouldering heaps of spoil from the mines; the whirring headstock gear might be the most prominent landmark; the houses themselves might, too often, be low, mean terraces; but still, in the great majority of mining districts, the mines were set within sight and sound of the country-side. Even the Black Country had not yet been absorbed into the spreading mass of Birmingham. The miners were not urban workers at all. Even now, if you travel round the different districts, you find the countryside and the mines closely intermingled. In the Welsh valleys, even in modern towns such as Merthyr, where glass and concrete have replaced the older buildings of brick and stone, you still find the country creeping in. The hill sheep wander down to take a tentative sniff at this new world, but soon trot off again. In the smaller towns they are much more frequent visitors, wandering unconcerned into the traffic of a main road as it slices through the centre of a narrow valley settlement. Perhaps this closeness to the countryside has helped to keep alive so much of the traditional way of life, so easily lost among the changing patterns and shifting flows of population in the big industrial towns and cities. Perhaps, too, this isolation helps to explain why a miner from Fife might have more in common with a miner from Pontypridd than with a closer neighbour. The common bond between them was to be sorely tested in the years following the First World War.

Opposite: Changing dress, changing age, changing faces: two centuries of miners and mining communities. A few individuals have been caught, arrested by pen and brush or camera to look out at us to represent the individual who goes down the mine to win coal. A Glasgow pitman of the nineteenth century.

Miner

Staffordshire pitmen.

Boys pose for the camera in the early
twentieth century, defiantly adult.

154

More boys crouch waiting until they're big enough to stand with the men.

A deputy poses, very dignified, in about 1900.

The Bevin Boys of the 1940s seem uncertain about their future.

155

Above: The men
go to work.

Left: The men
come home.

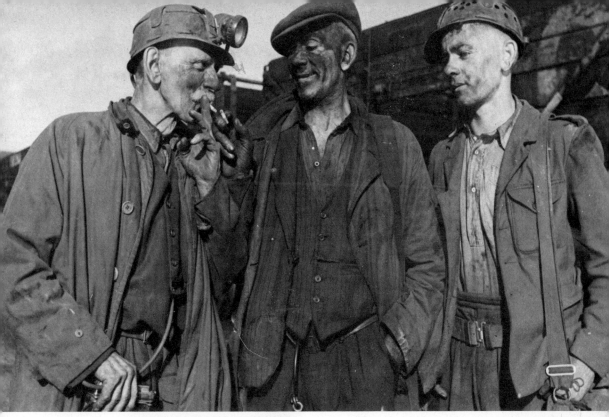

Top: Three generations of miners at Sengenhydd: John Thomas (sixty-seven), Sylvester Thomas (forty-one), and Donald Thomas (sixteen). Above: The young visit the old – and the young miner squats on his heels as miners have done for centuries before him. Right: Cheerful women leave the screens at Wigan.

Sitting, scarcely able to breathe, one of
the thousands of ex-miners whose days
will end with their lungs clogged and
rotted with the dust and filth of the
mine.

Less cheerfully, men bear the badge of
suffering, bowed with working the
narrow seams.

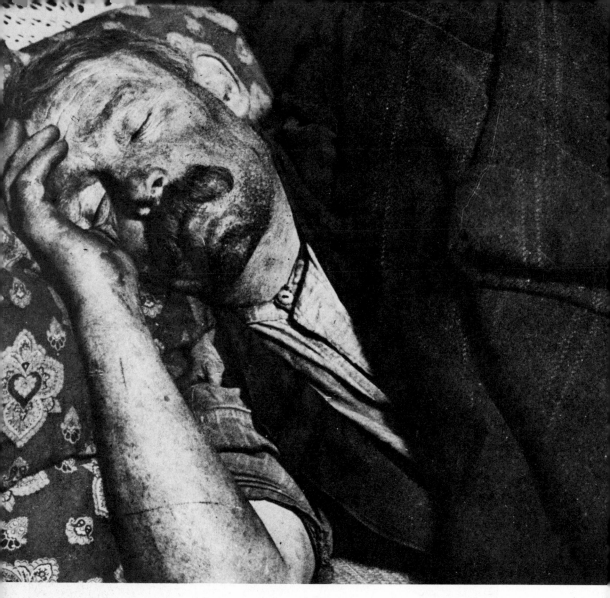

Work over, the old miner sleeps.

Chapter Ten

Depression and War

In the first heady days of war, men from all over Britain rushed to volunteer for the forces that were to crush the upstart Kaiser, confident that, having given the Germans a suitable lesson, they could return as heroes and resume their old lives. The miners were not immune from the general hysteria and cheerfully joined in the rush. But when the Government awoke to the fact that the war that was to be over by Christmas was to last a good deal longer, they also had to work out how to keep up a high level of coal production to meet the needs of war industry. In the first year of war, 250,000 men left the mines, and the Government were forced to interfere in what had once been a sacrosanct preserve of the private mine-owner. Decisions were now too important to be left to a multiplicity of small owners, and by the end of the war Government control had been so far extended that the owners were left with nothing but day-to-day management responsibility. For the men it was a novel experience: power had been taken away from the all-powerful owners by the Government. At the end of the war, the miners were better paid and had a new sense of belonging to the industry which gave them their livelihood. The men argued, not illogically, that if such a system was both necessary and successful in wartime, why should it not be equally necessary and successful in peacetime? At the end of 1918, the Government still had control over railways and mining and found themselves facing the old Triple Alliance and a new set of demands among which was one from the miners for nationalization. Threatened by industrial action, the Government set up a Royal Commission under Sankey, a High Court judge.

The Sankey Commission was another new departure: now miners and owners had to sit down together on equal terms to attempt to reach agreement on the future of coal. Perhaps no one, least of all the Government whose main interest was in avoiding a strike, expected agreement. If they did, they were disappointed. When the sessions finally ended in the summer of 1919, there was no more unanimity than there had been at the beginning: each section produced a report setting out its own views. These varied between a demand for nationalization by the miners, to a demand from the owners for a return to the pre-war conditions. Lloyd George suggested a compromise of reorganization. The miners were disenchanted with the proposal, and the owners indignant. Lloyd George withdrew his modest reform proposals and nothing at all was done. The miners continued their demands for nationalization, but the Sankey Commission was the last time such demands were taken seriously until after the Second World War.

The owners, in their turn, set out the case for a return to 'normality'. In a pamphlet, *What Mr Lloyd George Was Not Told*, they stated that 'the discontent with which, so it is suggested, the mining population is seething, is directly traceable to manufactured agitation and is largely due to the encouragement given to the agitators to fish in the troubled waters of politics . . . if the parties in the industry are left alone to solve their own problems they will do so'. The second supposition had even less basis in fact than the first. The pre-war conditions were coming back with a vengeance, both sides again set in stubborn direct opposition – it was a war not very different in its blind, unreasoning attitudes than that just finished. Lord Birkenhead noted sourly of the miners that 'I should call them the stupidest men in England if I had not previously had to deal with the owners.' Not a fair comment perhaps, but it gives an inkling of the very personal nature of the battle into which the two sides threw themselves with a passion quite incomprehensible to outsiders.

In the panicky years at the beginning of the 1920s, the Government hastily rid itself of the troublesome mining industry, handing control back to the old owners. The mines were already showing signs of decline, with modernization badly needed. But, alas, that was not a word much in vogue among the owners. Their response to economic difficulty was by now virtually Pavlovian: they ordered a cut in wages and a return to the old system of district bargaining. The miners demanded a national negotiating policy and refused to accept a cut. The sequence followed its well-worn route – the owners ordered a lock-out to begin on 1 April 1921. The miners now called on their partners in the Triple Alliance for support. The story of what happened in that month is muddled, interpretations are legion. In essence, the Government offered to mediate, to impose a standstill while negotiations continued. The Miners' Executive, after meeting in secrecy, rejected the offer after a good deal of argument. The other two parties were not consulted, but their attitudes were in any case very different from those of the miners. Ernest Bevin, leader of the Transport Workers, favoured conciliation and not the violent confrontations of the past. He favoured the miners' acceptance of mediation. It was a common-sense approach, but Bevin's union had not the same history of bitterness as the miners'. It might have been possible for him to sit down and trust in the good faith of the employers. Between miners and mine-owners there was precious little trust to be found. Whatever the rights and wrongs of the situation, the Railway and Transport

Unions baulked at supporting what they regarded as unreasonable obstinacy on the part of the miners and called off their strike. To the miners it was betrayal, and 15 April 1921 went down in their books as 'Black Friday', a day to be remembered with shame. Now they were left to themselves and they were defeated, the cuts were imposed. As so often in the past, the miners were in the front line and when that was broken a more general attack followed on wages in other industries.

The mining industry then went into one of its rare periods of expansion, and conditions improved until a booming European coal industry began steadily to remove Britain's coal export trade. The Pavlovian response was instantly forthcoming – demands for longer hours and less pay. The Trades Union Congress offered support to the miners, and the Government, faced by the prospect of united action, hastily found the formula to fend off disaster. They appointed a Royal Commission under Sir Herbert Samuel to look into the mining industry. A victory for the Trade Unions to erase the memory of Black Friday? Not quite. The Commission had certain basic disadvantages: none of its members knew anything at all about the coal industry, and they had no power to enforce their recommendations. In March 1926 the Commission delivered its opinion. In the immediate situation the miners were to agree to take less pay, and at some unspecified date in the future the industry was to be reorganized. The owners at once rejected reorganization, but accepted the recommendations for lower pay, adding a new demand for longer hours as their own contribution. The miners' leader A. J. Cook gave the men a new rallying-cry: 'Not a penny off the pay, not a minute on the day.' There were all the ingredients ready to be stirred into a very familiar mixture. But this time the T.U.C. was thrown into the pot as well. The miners wondered among themselves whether their supporters might not again find the fire too hot.

On 1 May 1926 the miners' lock-out began. The T.U.C. met the Cabinet and threatened a General Strike unless something were done for the miners. To the acute embarrassment of the moderate leaders of the General Council, the negotiations broke down. The General Strike was on. No other example of industrial action has ever achieved such fame in Britain. It was characterized by the totally unselfish attitude of hundreds of thousands of ordinary working people who were ready, with no prospect of gain for themselves, to come out on strike to try and ensure a decent living wage for the miners. For some, the General Strike had a much greater significance. For Winston Churchill, for example, it was a chance to engage 'the enemy', and he duly called out the troops and made an ostentatious display of power by ordering armoured cars to patrol the streets. The violent conflict never materialized, apart from some isolated acts. For the rest, it was more of a case of rather jolly fun for the undergraduates and others who turned out to drive the buses or satisfy boyhood fantasies by acting as engine-drivers. The middle class might have been nervous about the strike, but the General Council of the T.U.C. were even more worried by the powerful forces they had roused. At a meeting on 12 May, Sir Herbert Samuel suggested setting up a National Wages Board and pushing through a reorganization of the industry as a condition of approving a cut in wages.

The T.U.C. thankfully grabbed the offer. That it was unacceptable to the miners, that Samuel had no Government authorization but was only putting forward a suggestion were both overlooked. The General Council made no further demands, but simply called off the strike. The General Strike was at an end. The miners were back where they started. Yet it was a remarkable time – a dramatic demonstration that, whatever public opinion as expressed in the great majority of newspapers might say, the working people of Britain recognized the justice of the miners' cause. It was not their lack of resolution that brought the strike to an end, to be followed by the inevitable defeat of the miners.

Once again wages fell, hours rose, and with the rise in hours the rate of unemployment began to rise. As more men lost their jobs, so the bargaining power of the Unions declined and the standard of living in the pit villages of Britain went down with it. The owners yet again demonstrated their short-sightedness, using lowered wages to reduce costs forced up by inefficient mining by outdated methods. With the coming of the 1930s, the dark clouds joined to remove the last ray of light that might have given hope to the miners. The years of the Depression had arrived.

The Depression affected all Britain's workers but few were hit as hard as those of the mining districts. When, in 1934, the Government recognized the existence of what they euphemistically called 'special areas', the first four designated were South Wales, Tyneside, West Cumberland, and Scotland. But the suffering of the mining communities in the 1930s was not limited to them alone, and the story of their struggles during those harsh days is very little different from that of many other sections of the working class. The story has been told so often that it scarcely needs repeating. Names such as Jarrow, the town that suffered two-thirds unemployment, have passed not so much into history as into mythology. The hunger marchers who walked from all the depressed areas to protest for their right to work have become the symbols of that age. Perhaps because we know it so well, the age now has almost a romantic air to it. The marchers, among whom the miners were prominent, seem now to be so obviously deserving of sympathy that we might imagine that sympathy was what they received. But the accounts from the men who marched tell a more sombre tale. Will Paynter, the miner from South Wales, in his autobiography *My Generation* tells of harassment, of marches broken up by policemen with batons, of marches that seemed indeed to be headed for battle. But he also tells of the warmth and friendship, of the emotional scenes when the men from Wales came to Slough where many of their old friends and relations had moved in search of work, of the anonymous benefactor who treated the wet, hungry men to a fish and chip supper. In a way it was like the story of the General Strike: spontaneous support from other working people, and a Government unable or unwilling to give help.

The hunger marchers were the visible, dramatic symbols of unemployment, but the bitter realities lay in the towns and villages where the norm of life was no longer tied to the day's work but to the dole, where the means test left its ineradicable mark upon the whole community. The system of unemployment pay gave a fixed sum to a man out of work for as long as his insurance stamps lasted, but once they were gone the rate went down and the means test came into its own. It was a harsh system, harshly administered. A family with an old grandmother or grandfather living with them were said to have a lodger, and the allowance was docked by what the authorities considered an old man should pay out of a pension to his own family. To those who supported the test, it was seen as an attempt to prevent slackers or those who could afford to look after themselves, receiving money from public funds. To the unemployed the means test added humiliation to poverty, as officialdom turned its stare to an inspection of every compartment of their lives. It was loathed, and justifiably loathed at that.

For the fortunate who remained at work in the mines, life was little different from what it had been half a century before. For every pit that had mechanization, there were fifty that had not; for every new house with its own bathroom, there were a hundred terraces where men sat in zinc tubs before the kitchen fire. And all the time the old pits were seen to be less and less efficient, less and less able to compete with collieries in Europe and America. The multiplicity of small pits seemed as unlikely to change to modern methods as they had ever seemed. An atmosphere of mass unemployment was not one to encourage investment and dramatic changes in working methods. The policy of cheap labour proved as disastrous to the industry as to the men who worked in it. For too long, the owners had disguised inefficiency by using wage reductions to keep costs low. It could not go on indefinitely. In any case the need for coal suddenly became urgent as Europe and the world moved again towards war.

The war finally solved the problem of unemployment and, as in the previous war, the problem of the mines became one of finding workers not jobs as men left for the fighting. There was an attempt to recruit young men to the pits by offering mine work as an alternative to the services. The recruits became known after the scheme's originator, as 'the Bevin Boys'. It was an indication of general attitudes towards the mining industry that few could be found who preferred the coal-face to the front. Throughout the war, the industry hovered on the edge of disaster, with supplies just about keeping pace with demand. The peace brought a Labour Government and a mining industry with none of its problems solved.

Chapter Eleven

Mines for the Nation

The mines of Britain developed in the period we now call the Industrial Revolution. They developed and changed again, in just as dramatic a fashion, in what one could call their second revolution in the years following the Second World War. The first change was the most dramatic of all: centuries of private ownership came to an end. The mines were nationalized. There had been a century and more of the most bitter fighting before the miners even began to demand the ending of the old system of ownership, and decades passed after that before the battle was ended. No event in the history of mining has ever been more jubilantly received by the miners, nor has any retained a more affectionate place in their memories. Vesting Day was 1 January 1947. Then the day of the private owner ended. They went unmourned but not unpaid. £388,000,000 was paid over in compensation, a debt that was hung round the neck of the industry and that was to hamper its movements for years to come.

In spite of the jubilation of the National Union of Mineworkers, which had replaced the old Federation, the fortunes of the coal industry were at a nadir. In 1913 coal production from deep mines had reached a peak of 287,000,000 tons; In 1946 it was only 181,000,000. The industry was out of date, made up of a multiplicity of small pits, many of which were hopelessly uneconomic, and the need to produce coal had never been greater. Coal represented more than 90 per cent of the country's fuel and so coal was desperately needed if industry was to begin the recovery from five years of war. To add to all those problems, there was a chronic manpower shortage in the industry. Too many people had left in the grim years of the 1930s, too many had gone to the Forces. The mining districts had changed too little, the old terraces offered few incentives for men to return. There still lingered the smell of poverty that had filled the air only a decade ago. But the National Coal Board had no option: they pushed forward, as best they could, with an immense programme of reorganization and modernization, and with producing coal at any cost.

By 1957 production had risen to 224,000,000 tons, but there

was still no increase in manpower. Wages had doubled, but still the recruits did not come forward. The modernization programme was being pushed ahead but with the demand for coal greater than ever, the old pits still had to be worked with the unsatisfactory mixture of high cost and low efficiency. By the end of the fifties when reorganization and modernization really began to take effect, the whole situation changed. The new programmes had had their difficulties and these had been reflected in high prices, but it is sad and ironic that just when the situation might have improved the demand for coal began to fall. Oil was to be the new fuel for power-stations and for heating. Added to the move to oil was a decrease in the numbers of traditional coal-users. Diesel locomotives replaced steam locomotives on the railways, Clean Air Acts reduced the use of coal for home heating. From being told to work flat out, the miners found themselves exhorted to work less. They found, to their surprise, that their old demands for a shorter working week were not only being met but being enforced, as a halt was called to Saturday working. The great cut-back had begun.

The late fifties and sixties were a grim period for the miner. It was not the thirties again: there was not the same feeling of having constantly to battle against the owners for every penny earned, but there was a return to the gnawing uncertainty of those days. Would there still be a job to go to next week? Between 1965 and 1971 229 British pits were closed down. And in the vast majority of cases the miners co-operated. They accepted the case, however reluctantly, that the old methods had to go, that unproductive pits had to close. And they did more than that. Where, in a shrinking industry, the men might have been expected to resist the introduction of machinery that would take away jobs, the miners accepted automation. There might be little change to see above ground but below ground automation was becoming the norm not the exception. Power-loaders, which both cut and loaded the coal, were at work at the faces; armoured conveyors carried the coal to the shaft; hydraulic supports that advanced as the face advanced replaced the old system of pit-props. From being a skilled manual worker, the miner had become a skilled technician.

The co-operation of the miners in bringing change went even further. In 1966 the N.U.M. agreed to operate the National Power Loading Agreement (NPLA) which replaced district bargaining with a national award – something the miners had long wanted – but which meant some men had to accept a cut in pay. It also brought a levelling out of wages between the old élite of the face workers and the other men in the pits. The miners who lost pay recognized the justice of fairer sharing, but it did not alter the fact that when the NPLA was fully implemented at the end of 1971, some men had to go home with slimmer wage-packets. All these changes had the full co-operation of the workers and, at the same time, productivity figures had soared: from under 25 cwt per man per shift in 1951, output had risen to nearly 45 cwt per man per shift in 1970. No one could accuse the British miner of not playing his part in the re-vitalization of his industry.

The miners might quite reasonably have expected such efforts to be rewarded, but instead the wages of the miners were steadily dropping in the industrial league tables. Taking the average weekly earnings for manufacturing industry at 100 in 1967, the miners' pay stood above average at 107, by April 1971 this had slumped to 93. The position was absurd: productivity at that period had risen 20 per cent but income had actually fallen. The effect was inevitable. Men left the industry to get better pay for easier work and those who remained began to speak more and more insistently about pay rises. The days of co-operation were nearly over.

In 1972 the miners put their case for a pay rise and were turned down, not by the N.C.B. who were their employers, but by the Government who had instituted a statutory incomes policy. The miners were back in the fight and the national coal strike began. In the course of that strike, it really did seem that the years of co-operation between miners and management were being set aside, mutual trust steadily eroded, and neither side could stop the process. For the miners anything less than victory would be a sign that their industry had finally lost its place in the country's economy. The Coal Board was powerless. The Government stood on a point of principle – an uncomfortable position, and one from which it is notoriously difficult to shift anyone, least of all a government. So, in many ways, it was a return to the old days of direct conflict and the scenes that, in the days of television, reached every home were often violent. The pickets were determined that the coal should not reach the power-stations: there were arguments, scuffles, and fights. It was ugly to watch, but it marked clearly the way in which the mood of the miner had become embittered. Not that all the pickets were miners – a number of fringe political bodies saw the strike as a chance to make their own views heard. But the Government, faced by the threat to power-supplies, took a hasty reappraisal of its principles, and handed the question of miners' pay to a Committee of Enquiry under Lord Chief Justice Wilberforce.

The Report of the Wilberforce Committee has a double importance. For the miners, the first and paramount fact was that it virtually accepted the justice of all their demands. But it had another facet – it showed, in the evidence of individual miners, something of the way of life of the British miner in the 1970s. Here, for example, is part of the evidence of a forty-two-year-old miner, who had been down the pits for twenty-seven years, and now worked at Snow Hill Colliery, in the Kent coalfield:

'I am working in a pit which is much hotter than the previous one. Indeed, the men at the pit where I now work wear no clothes at all when working. This was unusual to me when I went there because I was used to working in short trousers, but eight out of ten men in the headings work with absolutely no clothes on because of the heat and, because of the amount of sweating they do, they have to drink a lot of water. Many, many men at Snow Hill Colliery drink eight pints of water a day and the Coal Board has provided them with salt tablets to put in the water to stop them getting whatever they are supposed to get by drinking a lot of water. . . . Since the advent of mechanization in the industry the amount of dust which is in the places of work has to be seen to be believed. Dust-suppression methods are used but in many cases they are not effective. I work with a dust respirator to stop the dust from going into my lungs but a number of men do not wear these masks.'

He had to travel an hour each way to work, getting up for the morning shift at 4.30 a.m. He says that in 1963 he was getting £5 10s a shift at the coal-face but that had reduced to £5 – 'in view of that you can probably see the feeling of the miners through me and the sort of attitude being expressed in the picket lines, and wherever you go as the result of the present struggle'.

The same story was repeated many times, though the heat described above was an exceptional circumstance. But time and again emphasis was placed on the effect of dust and the old miners' disease of pneumosilicosis. As another miner put it graphically, not in the Wilberforce Report: 'You end your days with a slab of coal where your lungs were.' For the men affected by the dust the situation was bleak. A forklift-truck driver, aged fifty-one, gave evidence of earning £18 a week with a take-home pay of £15. He had worked underground, but now his chest complaint had forced him to the surface. Yes, he agreed, he could get more pay working elsewhere at a similar job, but who wanted a man with a bad chest? The Committee heard the evidence and reached their decision. Point by point they went over the case. The conditions of mining demanded high pay; surface workers, the lowest paid, often had those jobs because their health had been broken working underground. In the words of the Committee: 'The British coal mining community is in some ways quite unique, living in isolated communities, often poorly housed, with mining the sole source of income.' They went on to summarize the history of the miners in recent years, their co-operation with mechanization and closures, their financial sacrifice. In the end the conclusion seemed inevitable as they agreed to the whole of the demands.

The problems of the mines were not solved by Wilberforce. It was not enough to give a simple pay award, the miners needed to be reassured that the industry was not again heading for decline, they needed to have their position reinforced in the wage scales of the country. Not until the miner could be assured that his job was safe and that his income would reflect the exceptional circumstances of his work, would the steady flow of men from the mines be halted. In 1973 the miners pushed again for a pay award, and again they ran headlong into Government policy. The miners' leaders sensed that there was still a feeling that mining was of secondary importance, an outmoded industry. The events of the winter of 1973–74 were to give a dramatic demonstration that mining was still vital to the whole country. The conflict began with an overtime ban. If the view of mining as an irrelevant industry was accurate then that should have proved little more than an irritant. Instead, to the astonishment of most people, the Government announced that the nation faced disaster. Industry was put on a three-day week and television told to close down early on the assumption presumably that the nation would then retire to bed forced back to older forms of amusement not requiring outside power. As the dispute continued, compromise and an end to the argument seemed progressively less likely. In an attempt to force the issue, the miners were balloted and voted for an all-out strike. Edward Heath, the Prime Minister, called a General Election on the grounds that he needed a mandate from the public to bring the miners to heel. The mandate was not granted. Harold Wilson formed a minority Labour Government, which promptly authorized the N.C.B. to meet the miners and negotiate with no Government restrictions. The dispute was at an end.

The strike of 1974 gave conclusive proof that mining was still a vital part of the British economy. The miners found an unexpected ally in the oil sheikhs of the Middle East, who suddenly announced a staggering price rise for their oil. Coal, still available in Britain, had seldom looked more attractive as a fuel, and the mounting trade deficit did nothing to reduce its attractiveness. So the matter stands: the coal industry is needed, the miner is needed. In the past 200 years the fortunes of the miner have waxed and waned. What he has gained, he has fought for. What he has won is his by right of work and struggle.